CLASSIC WALKS ON THE
North York Moors

by Martin Collins

The Oxford Illustrated Press

'Rest assured, you will not experience the
ecstasies in an easy chair by the fireside!
Tramping is an active delight which only
those who practise can rightly apprehend.
But up there on the 'tops'—away from all
books (and slippers), away from all sects (and
cities)—it is there for the finding. And every
man who tramps will find his own secret
crock of gold.'

A J Brown

This book is dedicated to Diana for her
patience and encouragement, and to
Paul in the hope that he, too, will one
day tramp the North York Moors.

With thanks to Richard Kreutzmann of
Colwyn Bay, Clwyd, for meticulous
processing of my colour film.

All photographs by the author.

© 1990, Martin Collins

ISBN 0 946609 99 3

Published by:
The Oxford Illustrated Press, Haynes Publishing Group, Sparkford,
Nr Yeovil, Somerset BA22 7JJ, England.

Printed in England by:
J.H. Haynes & Co Limited, Sparkford, Nr Yeovil, Somerset.

British Library Cataloguing in Publication Data:
Collins, Martin, *1941-*
    Classic Walks in the Yorkshire Moors. — (Classic walks)
    1. North Yorkshire. North York Moors. — Visitors' Guides
    I. Title   II. Series
    914.284604859

Library of Congress Catalog Card Number: 90-81555
    ISBN 0-946609-99-3

CONTENTS

INTRODUCTION

The North York Moors National Park was established in 1952. Its 553 square miles (1432 square kilometres) of heather moor, dales and coastline is roughly kidney-shaped, bounded to the south by the Vale of Pickering, to the west by the Vales of York and Mowbray, to the north by the Tees estuary and to the east by the North Sea.

About three quarters of the land is privately owned, the remainder belonging to the Forestry Commission, Water Authorities, the National Trust and the National Park itself. Administration of the Park is undertaken by a committee, 18 of whom represent North Yorkshire and Cleveland County Councils and local District Councils, while 9 are appointed by the Secretary of State for the Environment. Seventy-five per cent of funding comes from central government, 25 per cent from local ratepayers.

In common with that of other National Parks, the Authority's principal responsibility is to protect landscapes and wildlife. This is less simple than it sounds, for it involves reconciling the public's increasing use of the Park for recreational purposes with the interests of farmers, foresters and others who live and work in it.

There are few towns of any size within the National Park boundary, Pickering, Scarborough, Whitby, Guisborough and Thirsk all being situated just outside. However, many smaller communities will be found in the dales and on low land bordering the moorland block. The coast is more evenly populated and during the summer season attracts many thousands of holidaymakers.

On close inspection, a map of the North York Moors will reveal not, as one might expect, a single, coherent moorland massif of that name, but an accumulation of local moors often named after adjacent valleys or parishes. It remains an ancient landscape despite the encroachments of modern man—a landscape bearing clear signs of earlier settlers and industries. You do not have to be an archaeologist to recognise these relics or to appreciate their significance.

Rising to an average height of around 1200ft (366m) and reaching almost 1500ft (457m), the North York Moors represent one of England's largest continuous expanses of heather moorland. Whilst their elevation is unremarkable by mountain standards, the tops form a mini-wilderness which contrasts sharply with the broad, pastoral dales, forests, escarpments,

agricultural land and sea cliffs that flank them.

Main roads (apart from the A169 from Pickering to Whitby) tend to avoid the exposed and often inhospitable central moors, but a network of good, if tortuous, B roads thread through the dales and, in places, across the tops, providing scenic drives and a choice of starting points for walks. British Rail trains serve Scarborough, Thirsk and villages along the Esk Valley line from Whitby to Middlesborough, while the privately run steam-hauled North York Moors Railway operates between Grosmont and Pickering during the summer and off-season weekends. All in all, getting around the National Park presents few difficulties, though patience is sometimes required!

Happily for walkers, more than 1100 miles (1779km) of public footpaths and bridleways criss-cross the area; add to this all the green lanes, country roads and forestry tracks and you have ready access to one of Britain's finest walking regions.

Although a few up-market hotels exist within the National Park, the most common forms of accommodation on offer are inns and small hotels, bed and breakfast establishments, caravan and camp sites and youth hostels, the latter at Helmsley, Osmotherley, Westerdale, Saltburn, Whitby, Boggle Hole, Wheeldale, Lockton and Scarborough. The Ramblers Association publish yearly guides to bed and breakfast places and the National Park Information Service will provide a list of accommodation on or near the Cleveland Way.

Farms will usually take overnight lightweight campers for a modest charge, but in any event efforts should be made to obtain permission before pitching a tent. Details of formal camp sites are obtainable from the Camping and Caravanning Club of Great Britain. (All these organisations appear in this book under 'Useful Addresses'.)

Walking Conditions

Nowhere in the North York Moors are gradients or terrain particularly severe. Certainly you will encounter steep hills, bog and crags but they are exceptions rather than the rule. By exercising normal hillwalking judgement and given a modicum of good fortune with the weather, you are unlikely to get into difficulties.

The moortops themselves form vast sweeps of gently undulating country devoid of recognisable features other than the odd tumulus or distant corner of forest. Paths are frequently stony but can be boggy and wet where there

is an overlay of peat. Off these paths, deep heather, bracken and uneven ground—sometimes pitted with old mine and quarry workings—can make progress both tiring and mildly hazardous. It should be borne in mind too that the greater part of the moors is in private ownership and that technically you are trespassing if you stray from rights-of-way or concessionary footpaths.

Rough but motorable tracks built for grouse-shooting parties are not universally welcomed by the walking fraternity; they often link up, however, with old coaching roads, disused railways and ancient trackways into useful itineraries across otherwise difficult ground.

In summer, rampant bracken will obscure stretches of path, especially on the moorsides; under snow cover, paths can disappear altogether, heightening the need for navigational skills with map and compass. Although paths are gradually becoming better used as walking gains popularity, those in less publicised areas are still trodden by surprisingly few pairs of boots! Indeed, some map-marked paths do not exist at all on the ground! It is as if the moors have a capacity to absorb all who visit them so that even on busy summer weekends, freedom from crowds, noise and traffic is easily attainable by walking a mile or two from the nearest road.

Conditions in the dales and on lower slopes surrounding the moors pose different problems for the hiker. Wet weather mud in woods and farmland can be a nuisance, as can dense undergrowth during the summer months. Much of this more fertile land has been farmed for centuries; rights-of-way should always be followed carefully and gates closed, especially near stock.

On the coast, paths can be slippery and you will encounter a number of stiff gradients. Since the coast path usually runs along the extreme seaward edge of fields, extra caution is needed where marine erosion is causing the cliffs to crumble away: this advice is doubly relevant in windy weather or when young children and animals are present.

Weather

During the course of an average year, a wide variety of weather affects the North York Moors. In a winter blizzard, conditions on the tops will test walker and gear to the limit, while below in dense woodland, hardly a breath of wind disturbs the snow-muffled silence. Conversely, refreshing breezes in fine summer

Low Dalby Visitor Centre in the heart of Forestry Commission woodland.

weather will tempt discriminating walkers away from the heat and congestion of valley bottoms.

Using statistical data to describe local weather in detail can produce misleading results. British weather is, if nothing else, notoriously fickle and patterns are hard to predict with accuracy. During the same August week in three successive years I was drenched by torrential cloudbursts, besieged by mist and low cloud, and buffeted by strong winds beneath a clear blue sky! Nevertheless, in the belief that average values are sufficiently reliable to be of interest, the following information sketches in a broad picture of the North York Moors' climate.

Warmest months are June to September, with June the sunniest (6.1 hours daily average), closely followed by May (5.7 hours) and July (5.2 hours). June is also the driest month, though March is driest over the year as a whole. When assessing temperatures, it should be remembered that much of the Park stands in excess of 1000ft (300m) above sea level and will therefore be at least 2 degrees Centigrade cooler than general weather forecast values.

Wettest months are August (with an unwelcome 3.6in./91mm) along with November to January; a typical year's rainfall totals 40in. (1000mm). Some precipitation falls as snow, particularly on the higher moors where it often lies for more than 45 days, though wide fluctuations occur from year to year. The bulk of the photography for this book was undertaken in 1989, one of the mildest and least snowy on record!

In many ways, winds are of greater relevance to the walker than air temperatures. Nothing is so strength-sapping as making headway against a gale; if combined with rain or snow, conditions can rapidly become serious. Mean wind speed for the region is 8.5mph, with gales (Force 8 or above) on about 10 days a year. However, wind speed and direction are partly determined by local topography; some funnelling of easterlies occurs, for example, between the moors and the Wolds/Howardian Hills to the south, and to a lesser extent along Esk Dale in the north. Clues as to the commonest winds experienced in any one location are provided by the shape and distribution of tree shelter belts.

Well known for its 'bracing' air, the East Coast is exposed to winds from north-west round to east-south-east with a long fetch over the open, chilly waters of the North Sea.

Coastal temperatures will often be depressed during spring and early summer before the sea itself has had a chance to warm up, and winds of Force 6 and over are more likely than further inland.

From time to time, a 'sea fret' or 'roak' will roll in—dense sea mist caused by temperature differences between the air and sea surface water. Not confined to the coastal strip, this phenomenon will blanket the moors too, spoiling many an otherwise good day out and seeing you reach for your map and compass!

Equipment and Safety

Experienced walkers will, of course, be able to weigh up a walk's requirements, taking into consideration the expected weather, length of route, terrain to be covered and the fitness of themselves and others in the party. Those newer to walking, however, may find the ensuing notes useful and we would all do well to remind ourselves of the need to 'Go Prepared'.

Conventional wisdom about footwear has altered in recent years, paralleling the shift away from heavy leather boots. With choice now extended to include robust trainers, fellwalking boots, lightweight leather boots, plastic boots and sturdy leather shoes, it is less easy to pontificate or lay down hard and fast rules. In my view, well fitting, comfortable boots add immeasurably to the pleasure of walking. North York Moors terrain does not demand a heavy boot, but cushioning from stony ground, ankle support on uneven surfaces and a degree of protection from rain, snow, mud and grit are highly desirable. If you are travelling light in dry weather, trainers

would suffice, though it is all too easy to twist an ankle in rough heather. Gaiters or anklets are invaluable aids to keeping feet dry.

What clothing you wear will depend on the season and prevailing weather. In general terms, several thin layers are more versatile than one thick one. If you can afford them, there are excellent garments on the specialist market which 'wick' away perspiration, thus significantly increasing body warmth and comfort; other garments combine remarkably light weight with wind and shower resistance.

The body soon chills when you stop walking, so always carry one spare article of clothing. Cagoule and overtrousers are virtually indispensable for protection against severe wind and wet—a lethal combination which can lead to the onset of hyperthermia, even in summer. Winter expeditions over the moortops should always be taken seriously. Your gear and your own walking abilities need to be able to withstand potentially harsh conditions and even in benign weather safety margins—particularly daylight hours—are reduced. At such times, extra necessities include warm headgear, gloves, energy rations such as chocolate or dried fruit, torch and whistle, telephone coins, a survival bag, spare clothing, sustaining food and even hot drinks in a flask.

Winter or summer, other essential items for the rucksack are a first aid kit, map and compass and food and drink. Bear in mind when setting out that emergency gear may alleviate someone else's misfortune, not necessarily your own.

Common sense goes a long way in ensuring

the success of walks. Near populated lowlands there is little objective risk involved anyway, other than overestimating your stamina or getting caught out in bad weather, the consequences of either being easily dealt with. Longer distance hikes traversing the tops, however, require thoughtful preparation if you are to avoid an ignominious retreat or, worse, the involvement of a Search and Rescue team.

Exposure (hyperthermia) or sheer exhaustion, hand in hand with the demoralising effects of hostile weather and losing your way represents the worst scenario of all. Illness or injury can also lead to an emergency and it is at such times that decisive action will minimise delays in obtaining help. Write down the 6-figure map reference for the incident's location if possible and call the police by dialling 999 from the nearest phone; they will decide what procedures to set in motion.

Should you be the unfortunate victim, find as sheltered a spot as you can, put on all spare clothing (using a survival bag if carried), eat a little at regular intervals and make the International Distress Call—6 long signals (eg torch flashes or whistle blasts) each minute. The answering call is 3 signals each minute.

It is always prudent to obtain an up-to-date weather bulletin before setting out on the more ambitious routes (British Telecom's 'Weathercall' service is more specific than radio or TV forecasts) and to inform someone not walking about your plans. There are many advantages to walking alone—seeing more wildlife, determining your own pace etc—but going in small groups greatly enhances the safety element.

OS maps for the North York Moors region are: 1in. Tourist Map (ideal for planning), 1:25,000 Outdoor Leisure—South-West, North-West, South-East and North-East sheets. 1:50,000 Landranger Series—Sheets 99, 100, 101, 93 and 94.

Notes on Geology, Flora and Fauna

More than any other mode of travel, walking allows us to perceive the landscapes we pass through in an intimate, contemplative way. Stopping to gaze at views or to examine a pathside detail is the decision of an instant   a spontaneous act as much a part of hiking as putting one foot in front of the other.

It is not necessary to be an expert in geology to grasp the essentials of land formation and erosion, nor to be a botanist to enjoy plants or an archaeologist to be intrigued by antiquities. Specialists will, of course, gain greater understanding and insights than the rest of us, but even for the uninitiated the processes of observation and identification in the context of a walk are often reward enough.

Knowing what to look for undoubtedly adds colour to exploring an area on foot. A little reading up beforehand enables you to make more sense of what you see along the trail and enthusiasts may carry pocket-sized books, binoculars and other aids to extend the scope of their 'field work'.

A book of classic walks clearly addresses itself to describing selected routes and enlarging upon the intrinsic interest of each one as it unfolds. In this respect it is a book for those who consider walking their primary activity and there is neither the space nor justification for expounding at length upon the many environmental issues of relevance to the North York Moors. That said, I hope the following notes will whet your appetite for more information: books thick and thin dealing with every aspect of the region are available from local bookshops or from the National Park Information Service (see 'Useful Addresses').

North-east Yorkshire as we know it today has undergone a transition from sea and river bed to dry land lasting some 70 million years. The uplifting process has been a gentle one with no violent convulsions of the earth's crust to cause the kind of dramatic folding and buckling we

Newtondale (left), formed during the Great Ice Age.

see in mountainous country. Breaks and faults in the strata, such as they are, are most visible along the coast where erosion of shales and limestone (a startling 2in/5cm per year on average) lays bare the bones of the earth. Here, shoreline 'scars' of Lias limestone are exposed at low tide and coastal rocks yield many signs of their ancient origins. Fossils are abundant, especially ammonites whose flat, coiled shells, varied in form and pattern, reach occasionally to 2ft (60cm) in diameter. Whitby's town crest incorporates three ammonities, testimony to their widespread occurrence. Elsewhere, fossilised reptiles and dinosaur footprints were unearthed by quarrying activity during the eighteenth and nineteenth centuries and specimens acquired by museums across the length and breadth of Britain.

Under immense geological pressure, muds and silts laid down about 150 million years ago in the Jurassic Period were compressed to form the sedimentary rocks which characterise these uplands. Sandstone caps the high moors but has been cut through by streams, allowing the excavation of valleys such as Eskdale, Rosedale and Farndale in the underlying soft Lias shales. The same sandstone occurs as outcrops and crags, particularly in the north of the Park where they are used by climbers. To the south, the Tabular and Hambleton Hills from Scarborough to Helmsley, including the south-west escarpment, are formed from rocks of the Middle Oolitic.

Right across the moorland massif sedimentary rocks are all-encompassing, except for a narrow intrusion of basalt—a lava flow from 58 millions years ago. Known as the Whinstone Ridge, or Cleveland Dyke, it runs arrow-straight north-west to south-east through the Park and was quarried intensively for roadstone during the first half of this century.

Altogether more obvious than the esoteric complexities of the region's geological structure is its legacy from the last Ice Age which began 170,000 years ago and lasted until around 18,000BC. Indeed, most of the land forms which these classic walks traverse owe their existence to the effects of ice and meltwater, particularly the latter flowing from glacial lakes and rivers. You have only to travel on the North York Moors Railway through Newtondale or drive through Forge Valley on the way from East Ayton to Hackness to appreciate the titanic forces which once cut these impressive gorges.

Evidence is clear—in the sands and gravels left by melting ice, in 'erratic' boulders carried here from afar, in the sticky brown glacial clay deposited along the coast—that the North York Moors were besieged by ice sheets many hundreds of feet thick. During the course of the last Ice Age, the moors then desolate snowfields and tundra, there would be several advances and retreats of the ice before warmer conditions finally became established some 10,000 years ago.

Great forests of birch and pine once clothed the moors and although pockets of sessile oak and rowan still survive in sheltered spots, tree cover as such has long since disappeared. Changing climatic conditions, man's prodigious demands for timber, the clearance of trees for crop growing and extensive foraging by pigs, cattle and goats had already decimated natural woodlands by the end of the Middle Ages. It is a story repeated elsewhere in Britain's upland regions whose higher reaches, we now know, were not always empty and barren.

There are compensations! Today, 40 per cent of the North York Moor National Park comprises heather moorland and in late summer these high landscapes are animated by a glorious purple haze as bell heather, ling and cross-leaved heath come into flower. On fine days, brilliant patchworks of colour roll into infinite distance—another bonus, for views in the ancient woodlands would have been all but non-existent.

Without careful management the heather would fail to support its commercial populations of sheep and grouse. Each year only about 15 per cent of new growth is grazed and the remainder would rapidly become too dense and too tough to be of value. Both sheep and grouse feed on the tender young shoots which are encouraged by burning back mature plants each winter; patches of dense heather are left as shelter for grouse and their young.

During the summer months over 6000 beehives are installed on the moors. Each contains upwards of 40,000 bees, whose presence may not be welcomed by all walkers! Their industrious quest for nectar creates a soft background hum and in a successful year as many as 120,000 jars of rich, dark honey are produced.

Prolonged dry weather brings with it an increasing risk of fire to moor and forest alike. At such times it is incumbent on all of us to guard against dropping that smouldering match or glass bottle, for moorland flora may take many years to recover from burning.

Bracken continues to spread over rough pasture above intake walls and, in places, across the tops. It is an unwelcome colonisation which stifles other plants and indications are emerging that bracken spores may be harmful to man.

More exotic though no less persistent an invader, rhododendrons are gaining a foothold in many moorside locations. Parts of North Wales and Scotland are overrun by this hardy plant and the North York Moors could well succumb in the future.

Rarer plants occur in a few moortop localities, notably in the Saltergate and Goathland areas and in a protected enclave on Fylingdales Moor. In general, plants flower earlier on the sunnier southern and western slopes of the moors than on those exposed to the north and east.

Moorland birds likely to be spotted by the observant walker include curlew, golden plover, lapwing, kestrel, harrier and the less common merlin. Meadow pipit, skylark, wheatear, whinchat, crow and pheasant frequent undergrowth on or near the tops. Resident and migrant species share their moorland habitats with red grouse, but it is the latter's misfortune to be shot in the name of sport between the 'Glorious Twelfth' of August and December 10th: shooting butts are encountered widely on hikes

Bracken and rhododendron have colonised parts of the National Park, as here on the Hambleton Hills scarp above Kepwick.

across all the central moors.

Life in the sheltered dales is kinder and fosters species of bird, mammal and insect far too numerous to list. Exquisite wild flowers, herbs and grasses thrive in the limestone valleys, nestling beneath mixed woods of ash, birch, wych elm and sessile oak. In common with the rest of Britain, pesticides, ploughing, drainage schemes and the introduction of new grass mixtures threaten our less common native plants and many insects too. For the most part the dales are cultivated land and have been for centuries, witness the matrix of picturesque drystone walls. Farming, often a combination of sheep and arable, is a rigorous life and hard winters take their toll of man and beast.

Forestry Commission plantations occupy 18 per cent of the National Park. By and large, the communal huddle of 'battery' trees excluding light and life offers little of interest to the walker. However, forest tracks and rides do provide straightforward links between points, though you might need a map and compass!

With a dual role to produce timber and to create recreational facilities such as nature trails, picnic areas and forest drives, the North York Moors Forest District employs about 150 people and is administered from Pickering. Fast growing pine, larch and spruce—particularly the Sitka spruce—top the current planting league.

Stretches of water such as Gormire Lake, Scaling Dam and Boltby Reservoir are favourite haunts for ornithologists and botanists, while anglers pursue their sport mainly on the Rye, Esk and Derwent rivers.

Finally the coast, where active erosion of unstable cliffs and bitter winds deter the establishment of plants other than coltsfoot, common horsetail and other robust grasses. However, in sheltered hollows away from the sea are found primroses and yellow celandines and trees such as hazel.

The calls and antics of gulls, fulmars, redshanks, kittiwakes and cormorants provide a memorable backcloth to coastal walking. Robin Hood's Bay is a good, accessible location for viewing those birds and the waders which frequent rock pools and sandy shallows.

A history of industrial pollution stretching back over 100 years has left its mark on life at the margin between sea and land which here at the edge of the beleaguered North Sea seems less prolific than it should be. Nevertheless, two sections of coast are designated Sites of Special Scientific Interest, there being a further 51 within the Park, along with 10 Nature Reserves administered by the Yorkshire Wildlife Trust.

Historical Perspectives

Until around 8000BC, this part of Britain was virtually devoid of human life. Before then, following the Great Ice Age, fluctuations in climate and vegetation had rendered the area too inhospitable for man, though as time passed nomadic hunters from the Mesolithic Age periodically wandered over the moors, leaving behind them a scattering of 'pygmy flints'.

New Stone Age and Iron Age man had to contend with colder and wetter weather than today's: the moors would have been bleak and boggy indeed, with settlements and cultivation confined to low-level, sheltered locations.

It was the incursion of 'Beaker Folk' from the continent around 1800BC that heralded the Bronze Age and led to the development of food vessel pottery, so many specimens of which appear in local museums. The climate was growing warmer and drier, woodlands flourished, pasture and grazing land were good and grain grew successfully. Not surprisingly, Bronze Age man thrived and although few traces remain of permanent dwellings (they were probably not required in the then equable climate), signs of his occupation still represent conspicuous features in the moorland landscape: tumuli (locally 'howes', after the Scandinavian *haugr* meaning burial mound), groupings of cairns and stone circles.

Howes contained the bodies of more important Bronze Age people, along with skin clothing and other accoutrements. Over the centuries many of these burial chambers were ransacked and their contents lost forever; some of the worst offenders were Victorian treasure hunters who bought plundered material from unscrupulous grave robbers and kept no records of their booty.

Wade's Causeway, a fine example of Roman roadway, marches across Pickering and Wheeldale moors, but apart from mounds and ditches associated with the coastal signal stations, and Cawthorn Camp between Newtondale and Rosedale, relatively little remains from the Roman era.

When the Romans left Britain in AD410, a northward migration by Angles took place, but 200 years later there was still no widespread, permanent settlement of the northern hills.. However, numerous villages to the south, ending today in '-ley' or '-ton' (eg Pockley, Appleton) indicate successful farming there by the Angles.

Ninth-century Danish invaders accepted Christianity, stayed, and added their influence to place-names, hence 'kirkby' for church town and '-by' for a small farm or hamlet (eg Battersby, Ingleby).

Stone crosses—here intact, there mere stumps or socket stone and shaft—are a distinctive element in the moorland scene. Several are very well known, Lilla Cross, for instance, being the oldest Christian monument in northern England and Young Ralph Cross adopted as the National Park emblem. Their origins are shrouded in mystery. Some were probably erected by monasteries to provide spiritual reassurance for travellers, others serving as signposts near the intersection of important trackways, others still commemorating local worthies whose identities have been swallowed in the mists of time.

By the Domesday census of 1086, no less than 69 communities in the North York Moors region were important enough for mention. Within a century, great abbeys such as Rievaulx and Byland, established by Cistercian monks who found the isolation ideal for spiritual retreat and the development of sheep farming on the poorer uplands, would transform these remote, unpopulated areas.

Castles at Pickering, Helmsley and Danby repulsed raids by Scots from across the border and also helped control a population scattered in hamlets and villages throughout the great Royal Forest.

From the medieval ports of Whitby and Scarborough and from many smaller coastal communities grew a seafaring tradition that found its zenith in Captain Cook's voyages of discovery. As the photographs of Frank Meadow Sutcliffe illustrate, herring fishing thrived in the nineteenth century, but the majority of people looked inland to the moors and dales for their livelihoods rather than to the hostile and unpredictable waters of the North Sea.

Iron smelting, jet carving and other small-scale industry—even glass-making by French settlers in the sixteenth century—had been carried on in this part of Britain for several hundred years. Prodigious quantities of alum-bearing shale had been dug from the Cleveland Hills and the coast for use in the dyeing and tanning trades, until a cheaper alternative was discovered in colliery waste. The scars of workings at Boulby and Loftus, Sandsend and Ravenscar still deface the land.

In the mid-nineteenth century however, on the heels of the Industrial Revolution, the country's burgeoning appetite for raw materials resulted in a period of mining activity which would profoundly affect whole communities and landscapes. Though short lived, the extraction of ironstone from various locations—chiefly from Rosedale—spawned a vigorous industry. Vertical shafts and horizontal 'drifts' were opened up in the dalesides and railway lines constructed to transport the ore. An infrastructure of kilns, hoppers, chimneys, coal pits, cottages, railway sidings and trackside buildings sprang up. By 1870, when production was at its height, a railway line had been laid right over the moors, enabling trains to deliver their loads, via the cable-operated Ingleby Incline, down to Battersby and thence to the smelting mills of Durham and Teesside.

Young Ralph Cross — emblem of the National Park.

take all the outings described in these pages, your experience of this magnificent area would be comprehensive.

Walks vary considerably in length and difficulty, some being wholly suitable for young families or the less active, while others are aimed specifically at the fit and properly equipped hill-walker. Except for long-distance and challenge walks which have been established by organisations or individuals, all the routes are based on personal research and are unconditionally recommended. However, there is nothing to prevent walkers devising their own extensions, detours or short-cuts with the help of relevant OS maps. Rather than thinking of these classic walks as immutable, I hope readers will feel encouraged to explore more of the glorious countryside stretching to left and right of the paths I have chosen.

Notes on Photography

I had hoped for more snow during the compilation of this book; it would have lent variety and a little added interest to the illustrations, but 1989 was stubbornly mild! At least I was spared the problems of driving on icy roads and standing around in freezing conditions!

Apart from a few 35mm slides already in my collection, the photographs in this book were taken using Mamiya C330 medium format cameras. The need for black and white as well as colour meant carrying 2 bodies, along with 55mm wide-angle, 105mm and 250mm telephoto lenses. I invariably use a sturdy tripod to help in composing the picture, to avoid camera shake and to increase depth of field through slow shutter speeds and small lens apertures.

To determine exposure I use a Weston Euromaster with Invercone for incident light readings, combined with a Pentax Spotmeter which is especially useful for distant landscapes.

The colour temperature of daylight varies enormously and since lenses and film record colour differently to our own eyes, correction filters are sometimes necessary: pale brown, pale pink and pale yellow filters were most commonly used, mainly to reduce the blue cast produced by atmospheric haze and the effects of UV radiation. A polariser helped increase colour saturation in many of the shots.

I find Fujichrome 100 film ideal for this kind of mixed landscape work; it has good colour balance, enough speed to allow exposure flexibility and on 6x6cm size is virtually grainless.

The old railway trackbed is still there—used now by walkers—so are the ruins of winding houses, calcining kilns and other structures, fascinating reminders of a recent chapter in our industrial history.

Another, quite different, use for a naturally occurring substance centres round the carving of jet. Though greatly admired by the Romans, the peak of its exploitation was reached in the 1870s at Whitby, where over 1500 people were employed making ornaments and jewellery. Hard jet was valued more highly than the soft variety and carvers often specialised in their own subjects, such as fruit, foliage or heads. Changing fashions and cheaper Spanish jet sounded the industry's death knell around the turn of the century, but it had always been a somewhat precarious occupation, particularly for the miners who had difficulty locating and extracting the elusive jet in cliffs and hillsides.

George Stephenson brought the railway to Whitby through Newtondale, thus opening up Scarborough and Bridlington to mill workers starved of fresh air and sunshine. The line was axed by Dr Beeching in 1964 but lives on as a popular steam-hauled private enterprise.

Throughout man's occupation of this region,

an intricate web of tracks, paths and packhorse ways evolved in order to move commodities between markets, villages and the coast. With the advent of motorised transport here in the 1930s, some of these centuries-old byways were overlaid by stones and tarmac or lost through neglect. Many, though, remain intact and it is to our forbears who made them that today's walking fraternity owes a considerable debt.

About the Walks

A more accurate, though less elegant title for this book might have been 'Some Classic Walks in the North York Moors'. Indeed, there are so many paths, tracks and lanes in the National Park—so many permutations of possible routings—that a book twice this size would still risk omitting the favourite walks of readers who know the area well.

In keeping with the 'classic' tab, I have drawn together a collection of itineraries which exploit the best of the tremendous range of country embraced by the North York Moors, and which visit as many noteworthy features as could be incorporated. I do not claim to have mentioned every worthwhile path, nor to have represented every place of interest, but if you were to under-

9

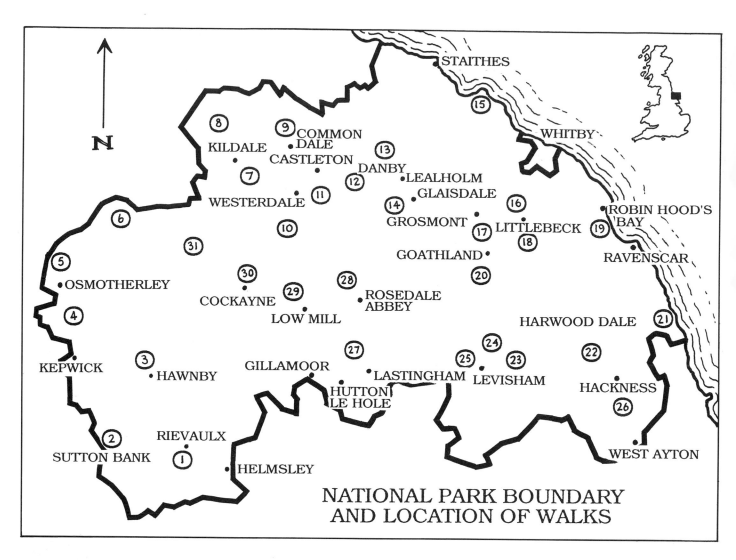

STAITHES

⑮

WHITBY

⑧

⑨ COMMON
DALE

KILDALE

⑬

CASTLETON

DANBY

⑦

LEALHOLM

⑫

GLAISDALE

⑪

WESTERDALE

⑭

⑯

GROSMONT

ROBIN HOOD'S
BAY

⑥

⑰ LITTLEBECK

⑲

⑩

⑱

⑤

⑯

GOATHLAND

RAVENSCAR

⑪

OSMOTHERLEY

③⑩

⑳

⑤

④

⑳ ⑳

⑳

HARWOOD DALE

②⓵

COCKAYNE

②⑨

ROSEDALE
ABBEY

KEPWICK

LOW MILL

②④

③

②⑦

②⑤

②③

②②

HAWNBY

GILLAMOOR

LASTINGHAM

LEVISHAM

HACKNESS

HUTTON
LE HOLE

②⑥

②

RIEVAULX

WEST AYTON

SUTTON BANK

①

HELMSLEY

N

**NATIONAL PARK BOUNDARY
AND LOCATION OF WALKS**

Facing page: **Helmsley Castle.**

**England's largest continuous expanse
of heather moorland occurs on the
North York Moors.**

WALK 1: *Helmsley Castle, Rievaulx Abbey and Old Byland*

Terrain: Undulating field and woodland paths, tracks and country roads. **Start/Finish:** Helmsley market square. **Distance:** 12 miles (19.5km).
Maps: OS Landranger Sheet 100; Outdoor Leisure South-West sheet.

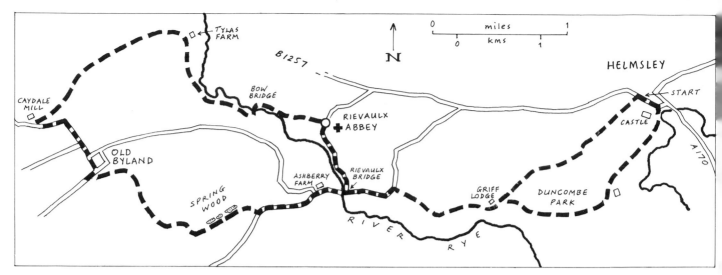

Visitors entering the National Park from the south-west often sweep along the fast A170 from Sutton Bank into the sheltered hollow of Rye Dale to reach Helmsley. At peak holiday times, jostling for a parking space and side-stepping flocks of coach trippers can mar your appreciation of this fine little market town, but early and late in the day it regains its composure. Both Helmsley Castle and Rievaulx Abbey suffer similar invasions during the high season, so choose your day thoughtfully if, like me, you value peace and quiet when exploring old buildings. Away from these focal points, the intimate countryside of Rye Dale remains undisturbed save for the occasional passing hiker.

Helmsley has not been slow to exploit its own picturesqueness and caters for a tidal flow of visitors with considerable *savoir faire*. Smart boutiques and antique shops rub elbows with traditional stores, yet neither the Yorkshire accent nor good, old-fashioned Yorkshire friendliness seem in any way diminished by such enterprise. Beneath the veneer of tourism I suspect that rural, small-town life continues much as it does throughout the rest of the year.

Food, drink and accommodation (including a youth hostel) are not hard to find and the National Park Information Service has its headquarters in Bondgate, just along from Market Square. West of the square, with its two crosses, ancient and modern, past the Town Hall Information Centre, stand the imposing ruins of Helmsley Castle; there is an entry charge but the site is immaculately maintained by the Department of the Environment.

Helmsley Castle was put up over a period of 40 years around the turn of the twelfth and thirteenth centuries by Robert de Roos, Lord of Helmsley. Many additions were made up to the 1600s, but much of the oldest masonry has gone. Following a siege by 1000 troops under Sir Thomas Fairfax during the Civil War, the castle

was honourably surrendered on November 22nd 1644 and eventually became a source of local building stone. Nevertheless those sections left standing are well preserved and are surrounded by formidable earthworks.

The walk begins opposite the church entrance, west along Cleveland Way— appropriately named, for it launches long-distance walkers on a route of that name across the moors to the North Sea coast. Very soon there are retrospective views from the walled track to Helmsley Castle above its manicured, grassy banks. After a succession of ladder stiles along field headlands above Blackdale Howl Wood, a waymark sign directs you into a steep and heavily overgrown little valley, to cross a track and climb out up steps. Ahead are concrete foundations—the scant remains of a World War II Polish Army Camp—then rough pasture leading towards Griff Lodge. Beyond the access track and before Whinny Bank Wood obscures your vision to the south, marvellous views open up over Rye Dale's water meadows and steep, wooded hillsides, and east back to Duncombe Park

Well walked as you would expect, the path hugs the top of Whinny Bank then ambles easily down through Quarry Bank Wood to a bend in the country road at Ingdale Howl. From here you walk left along the tarmac for some 800m and turn right at Rievaulx Bridge on a riverside lane for a further kilometre to reach Rievaulx Abbey. There is no denying the potential distastefulness of this short road bash should your visit coincide with an influx of car and coach borne sightseers. It is, however, unavoidable and you can at least gloat over the freedom walkers enjoy from parking problems and traffic jams!

Rievaulx Abbey's reputation as one of our country's finest ecclesiastical ruins is above question. Founded eight and a half centuries

ago, its majestic architecture on a valley site beside the River Rye is hugely impressive, even in an age such as ours, inured to large scale structures and grandiose architectural gestures. Everywhere is quality and harmony, from soaring walls, massive pillars and the symmetry of arch and window, to detail and texture at close range; the choir, in particular, is a superb example of the thirteenth-century stone mason's craft.

Lyrically situated near the junction of Rye Dale and Nettle Dale, Rievaulx was northern England's first Cistercian monastery—according to St Ailred in 1143, 'a marvellous freedom from the tumult of the world'. Outlying walls, foundations and mounds are evidence that the abbey originally occupied more ground than the present ruins at first suggest. A full history of the abbey's development lies outside the scope of this book, but it is fascinating to reflect that during its heyday 140 choir monks and over 500 lay brothers (monks not in holy orders) lived and worked here. At one time, the management of 14,000 sheep, iron working, fishing and salt production yielded great wealth and the monastic community thrived. However, towards the Dissolution of the Monasteries, fortunes declined and the house fell into debt. By 1536 only 22 monks remained: after four centuries of religious life, self sufficiency and considerable enterprise, the great abbey finally fell into disrepair and was eventually stripped for building stone. It was passed down to the Duncombe family, local landowners, being acquired by the State in 1918, and now managed by the Department of the Environment.

There's more! Tree-clothed hillsides above the abbey conceal Rievaulx Terrace from view, but this half-mile, flowery, woodland trail owned by the National Trust is worth a visit in its own right—perhaps on another occasion as the entrance is atop Rievaulx Bank off the B1257 road. Laid out by Thomas Duncombe in

***Rievaulx Abbey from Ashberry Wood
in springtime.***

1758, there are mock classical temples at either end, the Ionic one furnished as a period dining room, with an exhibition of eighteenth century landscape design in the basement.Views over the abbey ruins are often hauntingly beautiful.

Continuing now towards the red roofs of Rievaulx hamlet, a change in the walk's character is imminent as well known historical sights give way to the subtler delights of Rye Dale. You begin by taking a path to the left by a barn, signed to 'Bow Bridge', passing through two gates and along between hedges into riverside pasture. Building stone for the abbey was often moved by raft along a specially dug canal linking with the river and vestiges of this can still be made out nearby. Soon you are close to the river, flow-

ing prettily over flat rocks beneath overhanging branches.

A stony track is followed left to Bow Bridge, situated on an old packhorse route and surrounded by tall trees echoing to the low, insistent call of wood pigeon. Over the bridge you turn off right towards Hawnby on a grassy ledge between rampant bracken and cultivated fields. A stile provides access to a pleasant riverside wood and down through this our path meanders past oak, beech, hawthorn and alder, slippery where tree roots and little brooks intrude, or where sheep have churned up the earth.

Back on open ground, you cut across pasture at a bend in the river and climb a lane to Tylas Farm; it is a quiet spot with good views of pastoral Rye Dale scenery. Our way now swings west and runs through a dark corridor of conifers in Birk Bank Plantation, pathside verges dotted with wild raspberry and myrtle. Dropping through bracken, grassy slopes ahead above Deep Gill—a tributary of the Rye—lead on to Caydale Mill, but the certainty of a 'bridleway' is lost on rough, boggy pasture until the mill, now a private residence, is approached.

I once drove down the lane from Old Byland, bound for Murton Grange and Hawby, but the ford at Caydale Mill, feet deep and tens of yards long, was utterly impassable. Fortunately a paddle is not necessary as the route swings sharp left above the mill to ascend the quietest of country roads, accompanied by lovely valley views. Levelling off, it soon meets a wider road which leads down to Old Byland. Arranged timelessly round its village green, these neat cottages, farm buildings, paddocks and a quaint Norman church stand 3 miles (5km) back from the Hambleton Hills escarpment on the open dip slope. It is a gently swelling landscape of large fields—good agricultural land but high and exposed.

Monks from Furness Abbey settled here before moving on to found Byland Abbey on its present site 4 miles (6.5km) due south.

Turning right on the bottom road past Valley View Farm, you cross small, nettle-choked Hill Gill on the left and continue along field edges. At a gate, you enter Callister Wood, pass a sign for Nettle Dale and cross a stream footbridge. Straight ahead, beyond a copse, you reach grassy levels and another footbridge at Grass Keld Spring, where the Cleveland Way climbs south-west through pine trees towards Cold Kirby.

I have always found the next stretch—a track to the left called Bridge Road—to be quite delectable. It passes three small lakes beneath Spring Wood, sheltered backwaters frequented by waterfowl, framed by a gnarled tracery of twigs and branches, the enclosing hillsides reflected in limpid green water. Meeting the country road at a gate, you turn left and walk down Nettle Dale, past the junction at Ashberry Farm and on to Rievaulx Bridge. During winter and early spring when tree foliage is absent, it is well worth detouring up behind Ashberry Farm to a point opposite the abbey ruins; this tranquil view rivals those from Rievaulx Terrace but is free of charge, traffic and, usually, other people!

Retracing your outward steps to Griff Lodge, you could take a variant to Helmsley through the grounds of Duncombe House, though permission will have to be obtained from the Estate Office before setting out on the walk. Instead of skirting a wall on the left from Griff Lodge, keep straight ahead on the main track through trees and in 500m bear left on a wide surfaced roadway towards the imposing house, formerly the seat of the Earls of Feversham but now a private school. It only remains to pass in front of the building and walk downhill over a cattle grid, Helmsley Castle on your left, to the estate gates at the southern end of Helmsley.

Facing page: **Gormire Lake and the Vale of Mowbray.**

Helmsley Market Square. Small-town life continues beneath a veneer of tourism.

WALK 2: *Sutton Bank, Kilburn White Horse and Gormire Lake*

Terrain: Good paths along the open escarpment and through woods and fields below it. Parts are overgrown in summer. A couple of moderate climbs. **Start/Finish:** Sutton Bank Information Centre. **Distance:** 8 miles (13km)—allow 3½ to 4 hours. **Maps:** OS Landranger Sheet 100; Outdoor Leisure South-West Sheet.

Above: **Kilburn village
from the escarpment path.**

Left: **On Whitestone Cliff.**

In the west, the North York Moors fall abruptly to the Vale of Mowbray. There are no real foothills to soften the transition, no middle ground to moderate gradients. One moment you are at 900ft (270m) commanding a panorama over villages and an infinity of field patterns towards the distant Pennines; at the next, down steep woodland paths, you are walking beneath grey-gold crags of weathered limestone and out onto gently sloping farmland.

Escarpments are rarely dull places. Something about the sudden dislocation of terra firma, the jolt from one level to another, the aerial views, are reminiscent of flight. They are airy places too, snagging the smooth drift of breezes, deflecting gales and rain into upward-racing maelstroms. An escarpment is one of geology's more accessible manifestations, an obvious land form whose features are exposed and recognisable. Erosion, woodland, a lake and colonisation by plants and animals add variety and texture to this edge of the Hambleton Hills. Except where paths negotiate the scarp itself, walking is level and easy, providing endless opportunities to appreciate views or close-range detail.

The route described below forms a figure of eight and can be started from any point, or even split into two parts. Its fulcrum is the Information Centre and large car park at the top of the A170's 1 in 4 hill up Sutton Bank; a busy and popular entrance to the National Park. Housed in the Centre (which opens daily from Easter to October) are displays on the surrounding countryside, an enquiry desk, book and map shop, café and toilets.

Crossing the A170, and turning towards the escarpment edge, you take a broad grassy track on the left signed 'Kilburn White Horse'. Nearby stands a toposcope pointing out such distant landmarks as Richmond and Great Whernside, the latter 32 miles (52km) away to the west. The long-distance Cleveland Way footpath comes in at Castern Dike on its way from Helmsley to the east coast, but our way heads, for the time being, in the opposite direction outside the Yorkshire Gliding Club's grassy airstrip. All along the scarp, curving 'bays' of limestone cliff funnel prevailing westerly winds into powerful updraughts—perfect conditions for the launching of gliders.

Passing a Forestry Commission sign at a path junction, you continue along the escarpment lip, arriving before long at Roulston Scar, a vertical bastion of rock when viewed from afar and a magnificent vantage point. Iron Age earthworks and a crest of deciduous trees crown conical, pine-swathed Hood Hill directly opposite. Druid priests are reputed to have held ritual sacrifices on its conspicuous summit and legend associates it with Robin Hood's final skirmish. To the south and immediately below lies the picturesque village of Kilburn containing the workshops of Robert Thompson whose furniture and carvings are distinguished by the well-known mouse trademark. Fertile countryside stretches round towards the Vales of Pickering and York and in good visibility you will be able to make out the pale towers of York Minster 18 miles (29km) distant.

Meandering onwards, our path soon reaches the Kilburn White Horse, though from this angle you would hardly guess its existence. Unrecognisable from above—no more than a rough, stony slope shored up with timbers, its eye an island of turf—the horse is best seen from Carr Lane just north of Kilburn village and is visible from up to 70 miles (113km) away. You may be disappointed if your visit precedes one of the periodic dressings with white chalk, for the rock here is a lifeless grey limestone, unlike the carved hill figures of southern England.

At a bench beyond the horse's tail, steps descend to a car park where a stone tablet records that: 'This figure was cut in 1857 on the initiative of Thomas Taylor, a native of Kilburn. In 1925 a restoration fund was subscribed by readers of the Yorkshire Evening Post and the residue of £100 was invested to provide for triennial grooming of the figure.'

In fact, Taylor's design was excavated by fellow villagers, having been marked out on the hillside by children from Kilburn School under the supervision of their teacher John Hodgson. It measures 315ft (96m) long by 230ft (70m) high and occupies almost 2 acres.

From the car park, our route passes through a gate and along a wide green track through pine forest, trending right all the time and climbing gently before dropping to a track directly below the escarpment cliffs. Soaring beyond a screen of tree foliage and undergrowth, these vertical crags of split and fissured rock, bullied by the elements, appear hugely impressive. Eventually you fork right on an ancient, well-trod pathway climbing quite steeply. Known as the 'Thief's Highway', it developed as an escape route for highwaymen working the Hambleton Drove Road. The top is heralded by a wooden bench and your outward steps are retraced to the Information Centre on Sutton Bank.

Gormire Lake is the North York Moors' only naturally formed stretch of standing water and the second loop of our figure of eight walk passes above and beside it, revealing something of its rather enigmatic character. Crossing the Cold Kirby road, you follow Cleveland Way signs north-west along the escarpment—at first also part of the Sutton Bank Nature Trail. Views across the Vale of Mowbray are no less sensational here than above the White Horse. Indeed, those great celebrants of Britain's natural beauty, Dorothy and William Wordsworth, came here

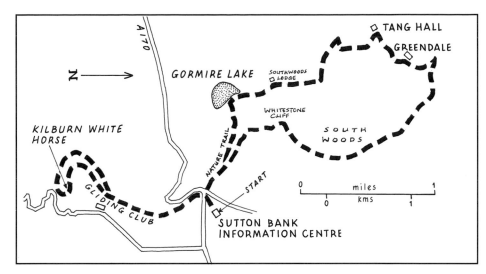

in the summer of 1802 to admire the wide vistas west to Great Whernside, Pen Hill and the gateway to Wensleydale.

Though seen well from many viewpoints, the deep waters of Gormire Lake are especially alluring from just beyond the point where the Nature Trail dips left. Cradled in bountiful woodland of beech, ash and sycamore, the lake is a favourite haunt of botanists. Reputedly bottomless, it is fed by underwater springs, with an outflow to the east which mysteriously disappears. Encircling paths are mostly private, but a special trail through Garbutt's Wood Nature Reserve has been established and is set out with numbered posts corresponding to notes in an informative booklet available at the Information Centre.

Before long you turn a corner to confront the undercut and sheer Whitestone Cliff, whose rocks belong to the Upper Jurassic dating back about 150 million years. During the Great Ice Age some 20,000 years ago, glacial ice hundreds of feet thick extended between these moors and the Pennines. Water escaping from glacial lakes to the north flowed between the ice and the moor edge—the line of least resistance—scouring channels along the hillsides and shaping the cliffs we see today. Gormire Lake was formed when a glacial landslip blocked one such channel below Sutton Bank and Gormire Rigg.

A mile of pleasant walking alongside arable farmland above South Woods leads towards the conspicuous tumulus of Windypit Hill Fort, but 100m before reaching it, you take a path slanting down a shallow gully on the left. At first between conifers, this takes you down by a wall, crossing a ditch to reach a rough forestry track on Little Moor. A gate leads out over pasture to a stand of deciduous trees and, beyond a stile, you descend through bracken beneath old oaks to a wall and sign post.

Boltby village is but a short step to the right,

but Tang Hall, our next immediate objective, is waymarked sharp left and in high summer this stretch of path is a struggle through rampant bracken until a gate brings you out into pasture above Greendale Farm. Keeping left of the buildings, the way follows a sunken lane in deep shade by a disused quarry and reaches Tang Hall farm.

Clear of the densely vegetated lower scarp slopes, the going is both easier and more absorbing, this time offering a 'worm's eye' perspective of the escarpment 'scars' and the lower outlying hills. An old green track and field paths take you to Mire Beck and thence to Midge Holm Gate and gently uphill beneath beeches to Southwoods Lodge. A 'Bridleway to Gormire' forks right over duckboarding through delightful woods. Gormire Lake itself tends to be tantalisingly obscured by foliage except during the winter months, reinforcing its secretiveness. It is a breeding place for wild duck, coot and the great crested grebe, serving also as a wintering ground for other waterfowl. About half way along the east shore, our way climbs steeply to a Nature Reserve sign and from now on follows the Sutton Bank Trail through self-sown birch woods. Many ferns, wild raspberries and honeysuckle thrive here, with bluebells and primroses abundant in springtime. Winding its way up the scarp slope, the path passes small-scale features too numerous to list.

Garbutt Wood Nature Reserve is leased to the Yorkshire Naturalist's Trust by the Forestry Commission and provides habitats for a wide range of plant and animal species. It is frequently visited by deer, foxes and badgers, though such shy and mainly nocturnal creatures are unlikely to show themselves to even the quietest passing walker. Emerging onto open ground, the climbing is soon behind you and a stroll back to the Information Centre concludes the walk.

WALK 3: *Hawnby, Dale Town Common and Easterside Hill*

Terrain: Mostly farm tracks and field paths, rough and possibly muddy in places. Some country road walking. One main ascent of around 650ft (200m). **Start/Finish:** All Saints Church, Hawnby, or the Hawnby Hotel. **Distance:** 9½ miles (15.5km)—allow 5 to 6 hours. **Maps:** OS Landranger Sheet 100; Outdoor Leisure South-West sheet.

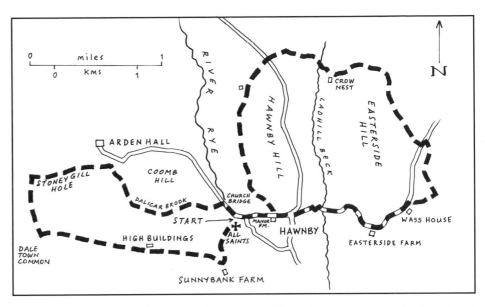

Hawnby, a village of many parts, spreads itself—inn at the top, post office at the bottom, church to one side—along the lower slopes of Hawnby Hill above the River Rye. A triangle of narrow lanes holds it together and even the roads connecting it with the outside world are unequivocally 'B'!

Apart from the welcoming bar at the Hawnby Hotel, there is little here to draw tourists who need souvenir shops, tea rooms and ice cream in order to enjoy themselves. Cottages of mellow stone at the hub of farmland and surrounded by hills, woods and unexpected valleys possess their own low-key charm. Prospecting this interesting route during mid-summer, I met no other walker, confirming how easy it is to get away from it all without entering 'wild' country.

Starting at All Saints Church near the western point of Hawnby's triangle of lanes, the walk forms two loops, either of which could be taken separately if a shorter outing is preferred. The church stands half obscured by trees on the banks of the River Rye. It has no features of special merit, other than a delightfully secluded setting, but come here in May and you will never forget the sight of tombstones engulfed by a sea of yellow daffodils.

Inside the building, an extract from the Yorkshire Herald of Monday, October 23rd 1916 declares Hawnby's 'Proud Record of a Moorland Parish'. Some 40 soldiers from the local community had already perished in battle and by the war's end the toll would be even heavier.

Car parking is not easy in the vicinity of Hawnby; wide verges near the church offer one option, the other being to patronise the Hawnby Hotel 500m away in the upper village and leave your car there! You begin by walking from All Saints towards lower Hawnby for about 100m then crossing the River Rye on elegant little Dalicar Bridge. You turn right alongside the river by a wire fence at first, but soon swing uphill by a tributary stream.

To gain the Hambleton plateau you have around 650ft (200m) to climb, steepest initially then easing off. Crossing a stile and an old green trackway, you follow the stream straight uphill, transferring to its west bank then turning left through a gate to join a lane from Sunnybank Farm, in view close by.

With both gradient and terrain relenting, you walk right, up past copses and thickets above North Bank Wood, ignoring a left fork and passing through a gate. Most of the ascent is now behind you and superb, far-reaching panoramas are opening up in every direction.

The barns at High Buildings, used for sheltering beef cattle in winter, are, predictably, besieged by mud. At my last visit they were also showing signs of severe wind damage—a persistent problem, I imagine, on this exposed plateau. Passing to the left, you continue ahead on a clear field track which, beyond a gate and small ruin, becomes increasingly overgrown and rough underfoot where stones have been cleared to the headlands.

This is cereal farming country, though I have seen oil seed rape grown hereabouts too. Alkaline soil conditions that allow arable crops to be successfully harvested here at 1000ft (300m) above sea level are due to an outcropping of Hambleton Oolite, but at the next gate you reach the limit of cultivated land. Ahead lies a very different landscape of heather and rough grasses punctuated by solitary trees and the hard, distant edges of forestry plantations.

Culminating to the north in the swelling summit of Black Hambleton, these stretches of moorland around Dale Town Common always strike me as being the wildest parts of the otherwise friendly Hambleton Hills. Although traversed by the Hambleton Drove Road (see Walk 4), relatively few other pathways venture across them and in mist or storm they are as inhospitable as anywhere in the North York Moors.

At the intake wall, you turn right and walk for about 800m over to a wooden gate where a path from the old stony Kepwick Road (an ancient thoroughfare never adopted as a modern motor road) comes in from the west. To your right, a path drops into the secret upper recesses of Stoney Gill Hole, a dale in miniature. The going is quite rough to begin with and in summertime you will be pushing through nettles and bracken, but beyond a spring the little gorge widens into a bowl of open pasture.

Coomb Hill rears its symmetrical, afforested head, while to the north, out of sight but only 200m away over a spur of Thorodale Wood, stands Arden Hall, a mainly seventeenth-century building on the site of a nunnery 500 years older. Downhill, you veer right onto a firm cart-track, ignoring an inviting gateway into Nag's Head Wood and continuing instead round the sylvan valley of Dalicar Brook, often echoing with the rattling call of pheasants.

Past a gate, the track deteriorates, rising and falling through cattle pasture. Where it swings away uphill, you take the sunken way alongside Carr Woods and walk down to the road at Church Bridge. Cross it as if to return to All Saints Church (which is, of course, an option), but take the left road fork up to Manor Farm. Opposite, a gate leads you up a good track. As it meanders through fields, there are impressive views ahead of Hawnby Hill's rugged western slopes and back to Coomb Hill, still a conspicuous feature. Forking right, the main track passes through gates alongside a plantation and reaches Hill End House.

From a fence corner where the onward track has become grassier and less well used, you must watch for a thin trod path veering half-right over open hillside. In good visibility you will be aiming just to the right of the Bilsdale transmitting mast on the distant skyline; in mist, you should be walking just east of north! Views broaden out again as the northern end of Hawnby Hill is skirted. From this angle it appears as a steep-sided hump—a hogback created by glacial scouring and almost a clone of neighbouring Easterside Hill.

Leading you round above a small conifer plantation at Moor Gate, the path reaches the Hawnby to Osmotherley road, where a cattle grid is crossed and an immediate right turn taken at a track intersection. Though less high than the Hambleton plateau by some 300ft (100m), a sterner moorland ambience prevails here on the threshold of high ground sweeping north to the Cleveland Hills escarpment.

The valley of Ladhill Beck demonstrates graphically how a changing economy, the rejection of traditional husbandry and problems of access can result in the total abandonment of farmland. Old field boundaries still exist south from the valley's upper reaches, but except around Hawnby itself, land and farmsteads lie derelict.

Further down the track from the moor road, a wooden post marks the point to fork right across heather to a double stile at a field angle. Crossing into marshy pasture, the way is not at all clear on the ground, but by keeping well to the left and aiming towards the northern end of Easterside Hill, you will come to a groove leading through a wall gap between low trees. It heads down to a 'V' shaped field bottom in the wooded valley, accompanied by an old wall; among the trees you will find a wooden footbridge—the key to this neglected section of the route.

Over the beck you take a rising line across an earth track, slanting left up to Crow Nest Farm. It was tumbledown at my last visit, but such properties have enormous potential and I would be far from surprised to learn of its acquisition in the future by someone prepared to undertake the extensive renovation work necessary to render it habitable again.

A handgate to the left of the ruin leads out to an edge of heather moor by a substantial wall. Walking up beside it, good retrospective views of Hawnby Hill are gained, as well as wide vistas to the north-west over Arden Great Moor, Snilesworth Moor and the hills flanking Bilsdale.

The wall is followed to its highest point adjacent to Pepper Hill—in effect the northern buttress of Easterside Hill—and round through heather above Bilsdale and the River Seph. Served by the B1257—quite a major road for these parts—Bilsdale's farms are securely 'on the map'; the transition from rough heather moor grazed by sheep to fields, trees and farm below the intake wall is clear to see from this elevated spot halfway up Easterside Hill.

The path really does afford very pleasant going! About 300m past a diversion avoiding an overgrown quarry, it dips gently, crosses a stile and a small paddock and reaches Easterside Lane. It would be perfectly feasible to take to the road here, but tarmac is anathema to most walkers and dodging passing traffic is not much fun either! Sixty metres along to the left you can escape by crossing a stile opposite and slanting back below road level. Following the bottom of fields, you eventually join an earth track from Grimes Holme which takes you up by a field fence towards trees. At a level with Wass House, you cross a stile on the left then turn right between sheds to find an old track doubling back to rejoin Easterside Lane.

Unfortunately there is no alternative to a road walk of about a mile (1.5km) to reach Hawnby Hotel—a little further if your car is at All Saints Church. As roads go, however, it is immensely entertaining. Just beyond Easterside Farm, the entire length of Hawnby Hill is revealed, its narrow, north-to-south profile the product of glacial friction during the last Ice Age. Easterside Hill, now seen end-on, appears as a rounded dome up to the right.

Dropping and climbing extravagantly (for a motor road) to negotiate Ladhill Beck, Easterside Lane joins the Osmotherly road near a telephone kiosk in upper Hawnby. Keep straight on at the village centre for the Hawnby Hotel (100m) and All Saints Church (750m).

Left: **Hawnby Hill from Crow Nest.**

Facing page: **The Drove Road over Black Hambleton.**

WALK 4: *The Hambleton Drove Road and Escarpment Villages*

Terrain: Forest and moorside paths (muddy if wet), a broad stony drove road and quiet country lanes. An ascent of almost 800ft (240m) is involved from Oak Dale to Black Hambleton. **Start/Finish:** Nether Silton. **Distance:** 12 miles (19km)—allow 5 to 6 hours. **Maps:** OS Landranger Sheets 99 and 100; Outdoor Leisure South-West sheet.

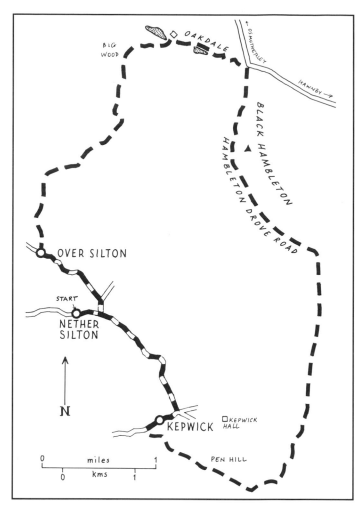

Top left: **In upper Oak Dale.**

Left: **On Black Hambleton summit.**

Facing page: **Kepwick and the Hambleton Hills escarpment from the path off Pen Hill.**

The Hambleton Hills escarpment, a convoluted and often wooded one overlooking the Vale of Mowbray and the distant Pennines, is traversed along its entire length by the Hambleton Drove Road. Although now metalled in places, substantial stretches remain in their original state—broad, rutted and stony—providing a perfect route for walkers.

It is quite feasible to walk any of these stretches from end to end, but more elaborate transport arrangements become necessary. In any case, taken on its own, the Drove Road might strike some as being a trifle dull: underfoot conditions vary little and gradients are few and far between. Not only does the walk described below paint a multi-faceted portrait of the Hambleton Hills—from below, from their

flanks and from the tops—but the section of Drove Road incorporated is generally considered to be the most dramatic and rewarding one.

A scattering of pretty villages connected by winding lanes below the scarp makes a striking contrast with conditions on the bleak moortops rising to the east. There is roadside parking at Nether Silton (easily reached from the A19) and at its pub, but care is needed to avoid obstructing residents and farm machinery using the narrow roads. The walk can, of course, be started anywhere, but easy terrain and the prospect of refreshments make for a pleasant conclusion here.

You walk east from the village for about 300m before turning left along Kirk Ings Lane and

by keeping left at a fork this little-used lane will take you to Over Silton. Here, a cul-de-sac heads north, past a telephone kiosk, and enters Forestry Commission land as a bridleway to Thimbleby.

Forestry plantations are not my favourite places. Without adequate waymarking or the accurate use of a compass, it is all too easy to become disorientated; vision is limited and felling can affect paths. Thimbleby Bank, however, is not large enough to swallow you without trace, though it is necessary to arrive at the correct exit point on Thimbleby Moor.

To achieve this you ignore the first track on the right, pass a gate and at the next junction take the left of three tracks—an earthy one climbing round in forest. A right fork puts you on a northerly course above the unseen Hanging Stone, and a further left fork, slightly downhill, brings you round to welcome, open views across Thimbleby and Osmotherley villages and 20 miles (32km) of agricultural plain.

Complications will soon be over! From the next track junction you take a less distinct, rather marshy ride on the left which quickly improves to a pleasant path, narrowing through bracken and rowan before mounting a rocky outcrop and emerging at a good forest trail. 'Landowners welcome Caring Walkers' is a considerable improvement upon the 'Private—Keep Out!' mentality which still blights surprisingly large tracts of open country. You turn left and reach open moor at a fence and, a little lower down, a stile.

At the time of writing, little flags on poles mark the onward path—not the most durable form of waymarking!—as you contour over rough heather and grass. Soon you enter Big Wood and, swinging right through bracken, will notice the swelling heights of Black Hambleton to the south-east. Dropping more steeply through broad-leaved woodland, a refreshing change from conifers, you cross Oakdale Beck's footbridge, aim to the left of Oak Dale House and turn right up a firm track.

This is part of the long-distance Cleveland Way (though you are walking in the opposite direction to normal) and if weather or circum-

stances suggest a retreat to civilised comforts rather than an ascent to high, exposed moorland, then Osmotherley's fleshpots lie but a mile or so down to the west!

Beyond a ladder stile, you pass the higher of Yorkshire Water Authority's two reservoirs in Oak Dale. They are secluded, intimate reservoirs, quite unlike the vast flooded valleys of mid-Wales, Derbyshire or Northumbria. At the far end, Jenny Brewster's Gill babbles musically through a shady copse.

First over duckboarding laid across vulnerable marshy ground, the way then takes you up a steep, well-walked track leading out to a bend in the Hawnby-Osmotherley moor road. For a mile to the left, past the Chequers farm and café which began life as a drovers' inn, the Hambleton Drove Road is surfaced. However, north from Solomon's Temple where the B road swings away to Osmotherley, it reverts to its authentic character—a rough trackway known as High Lane—before becoming metalled once again at Scarth Nick.

There is no mistaking the Drove Road heading south up the slopes of Black Hambleton. My last visit was in early June when bracken and ling clothed the moors with an uncharacteristic luminescent green. Colours are usually much more sombre, though the purple flowers of heather brighten August and September.

On a gently rising gradient, you now take to the Drove Road itself. Water drainage and the passage of countless feet have worn deep gullies: it is a difficult process to halt. Eroded footpaths become watercourses during heavy rain and lead, in turn, to new path lines being established. At a corner of forest, you pass a bridleway to Nether Silton—a short-cut if one is needed of just under 2 miles (3km) back to the start.

The advantages of gaining height soon become evident and it is well worth pausing now and again to admire ever widening horizons. Curious skyline humps to the north belong to summits on the Cleveland Hills escarpment, while to the west, forest-covered moorland gives way to a stunning panorama over the Vale of Mowbray.

A pile of stones marks the top of the heavily grooved trackway and on the left a double-rutted trod leads north-east to the rustic OS pillar on Black Hambleton, 1309ft (399m) above sea level. The hill's rounded summit limits views, but you can stroll north to Hambleton End to gain the best ones.

The Drove Road now snakes ahead over level, heather-clad terrain with a substantial wall on the right. Those amongst us of modest stature will snatch only glimpses of the magnificent westerly views where sections of wall have tumbled down! After some 800m, the way

swings sharp right alongside the wall at a private track on the left; from here onwards the Drove Road, increasingly grassy, widens to motorway width and you may well encounter horses out for a gallop.

Striding out in these fine open spaces frees the mind to ponder the history of this old thoroughfare. Drove roads and green lanes, we know, were mostly established in medieval times, though some could lay claim to prehistoric origins. Many survive throughout Britain's more remote regions. They arose principally, as their name suggests, from the need to drive sheep and cattle to markets serving expanding centres of population.

During the early years of the Industrial Revolution, demand for meat far exceeded the delivery capacity of an inadequate road system, not designed anyway to transport stock, and an as-yet undeveloped rail network. Animals were driven south from Scotland and even the Outer Isles, grazing along the way and tended by a hardy breed of drovers who had to deal with adverse weather, attacks by thieves, disease and the responsibility for good selling prices. Farmers along the way sometimes erected walls to prevent the travelling herds from grazing their hard-won, improved land either side of the drove roads.

Entering the National Park from the north at Scarth Nick, the Hambleton Drove Road climbs onto Osmotherley Moor and crosses the shoulder of Black Hambleton before levelling off along the escarpment, descending to Oldstead and Coxwold and continuing across the Vale of York. Packhorses carrying lime, iron and other commodities also used the road, for while carriages, coaches and wagons increasingly turned to the new turnpike roads, these old ways across the hills offered toll-free transportation, even if their unmade surfaces and exposure to the elements gave rough going.

Beyond disused quarries, you pass gateways through an enclosed section of the Drove Road. Limekiln House once stood hereabouts, a wayside inn at the centre of the lime-burning and distribution trade; it catered for thirsty quarrymen as well as passing drovers. There were other inns, too, beside the Hambleton Drove Road. Chequers, now a farm and café, was mentioned earlier; Dialstone Inn, also a farmhouse, stands just north of Sutton Bank; the Hambleton Hotel on the A170 east of Sutton Bank is the only surviving hostelry.

Never adopted as a modern motor road, the old stony way between Hawnby and Kepwick crosses from east to west. Still part of the Cleveland Way, our route continues straight ahead, passing a boundary stone and a couple of gates. Here you must watch carefully for a thin path leaving south-west over flat ground,

particularly if walking in poor visibility. Keeping right of a conspicuous tumulus and OS pillar at 1227ft (374m), it drops down the scarp slope near Clarke Scars in a sunken groove towards a wall corner at Gallow Hill. This reference to the summary justice meted out to cattle thieves and highwaymen is inclined to tarnish any romantic notions we may foster about life in those less bureaucratic days!

Further down, bracken gives way to heather as you converge with the great sweep of Cowesby Wood on Black Hill. Down to the right, Kepwick Hall nestles in the shelter of Eller Beck valley. Dwarf silver birch then heather, bilberry and the ubiquitous bracken line the path as you veer gradually away from the flanking wall and down a deeply worn trench on Pen Hill. Views of the under-escarpment, good, rich farmland for the most part, appear behind the exotic pink blooms of rhododendrons. Given suitable conditions, this hardy shrub grows like a weed and is already colonising areas of British upland to an extent that is cause for concern.

Passing beneath Atlay Bank Crags, you walk down a lush field path to a gate and the country road at Kepwick. Turning right through the village and left at the end brings you onto Bridge Beck Lane, twisting and undulating for a pleasant couple of miles back to Nether Silton. For most of the way the escarpment is in sight, culminating in a now distant, dark silhouette of moorland.

Facing page: **Set on a natural shelf below the moors, Osmotherley makes a good base for exploring the Hambleton and Cleveland Hills.**

WALK 5: *Osmotherley, Scarth Nick and Beacon Hill*

Terrain: Easy tracks and paths through forest and over moorland, with a little road walking. **Start/Finish:** Osmotherley market cross. **Distance:** 5½ miles (9km)—add 2 miles (3km) total for detours to the priory and chapel. **Maps:** OS Landranger Sheets 93, 99 and 100. Outdoor Leisure South-West and North-West sheets.

As the crow flies, it is not far to Middlesborough and industrial Teesside, nor to the constant rumble of traffic on the A19 trunk road, yet Osmotherley remains almost quintessentially rural. In a picturesque, flowery and perhaps slightly self-conscious way, it has managed to side-step the proliferation of tea rooms, gift shops and car parks to which so many pretty places submit. You either go there to enjoy its sleepy, old fashioned ambience or, as many do, you pass through while exploring the surrounding countryside.

Once an important market town, Osmotherley's streets of darkened stone houses are set on a natural, mid-level shelf, aloof from both the Mowbray plain and the high, exposed moors to the east. The church contains fragments of Saxon crosses, tenth-century 'hogsback' stones and a fine Norman doorway—testimony to a long history of settlement—while nearby at the village crossroads stand the ancient market cross and a stone table upon which produce was displayed for sale. Opposite, down a narrow alleyway, is one of England's earliest non-conformist chapels, built in 1754 following a visit by John Wesley.

The walk starts from the market cross, uphill past Mr Bainbridge's General Store and along Quarry Lane to where an access road forks down right for the camp site and youth hostel. Beyond the hostel, a track leads ahead to a gate, past the ruins of Cote Garth on your left and up alongside a stream in conifer forest.

You soon come up to the northern end of Green Lane, an offshoot from the Osmotherley to Hawnby moor road, and by turning left here you will find the quietest of forest rides, flanked by old broken walls. Though this plantation running down to Cod Beck Reservoir is a small one, its secret, breath-holding depths remain largely untrodden by man.

After passing a small stream, you emerge from the trees at a ladder stile and take a path on the left down by the plantation wall. In truth, there are so many trods in the vicinity that it is hard to describe the best line accurately. This is Sheepwash, an area of hollows and hillocks by the meanderings of Cod Beck. As its name suggests, here was a watering hole for sheep and cattle travelling south from Scotland and about to negotiate the high level Hambleton Drove Road to Malton or York (more about this in Walk 4). These days it has become a popular moorland halt for motorists and picnickers, though inclined to resemble Blackpool Beach on fine summer weekends!

Grassy levels by the beck lead on north-east to a more obvious car park and a footbridge, where the line of the Drove Road has been adopted as part of the B road leading down to Swainby. Tarmac is never the chosen surface of

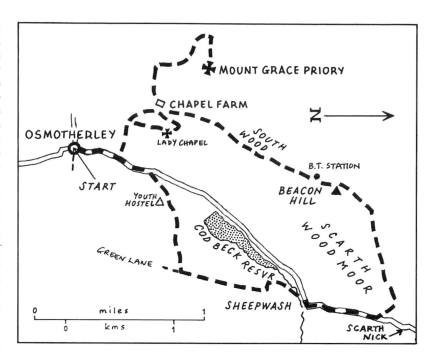

walkers, but there is distraction in your surroundings. Scarth Nick, towards which we are heading, is a narrow notch in the escarpment created by glacial meltwater at the end of the last Ice Age. No more than half a mile brings you to a cattle grid where the road drops away steeply to the agricultural plain.

Here the main walking thoroughfare along the Cleveland escarpment crosses from east to west and this route is now followed to the left (west) onto Scarth Wood Moor, with marvellous retrospective views. Rising gently, you reach two gates and continue alongside a wall above Arncliffe Wood to the OS pillar at 981ft (299m) on Beacon Hill.

A short distance farther on, aerials and dishes sprout futuristically from a British Telecom transmission booster station.

Waymarked 'Cleveland Way', the path now dips, spasmodically at first, into South Wood, emerging lower down to join a cart track through fields. Having descended easily to Chapel Wood Farm, you are presented with three options: to proceed straightforwardly via Rueberry Lane back to Osmotherley village (about 20 minutes away), to cut back sharp left just above the farm and visit the Lady Chapel, or to detour to Mount Grace Priory, adding about 1½ miles (2.5km) and 360ft (110m) to the walk.

If you've time and energy to spare, I recommend the latter, though at my last visit the way was less clear on the ground than it should be. Partly paved, a path leads down south-west from the farm, follows a field boundary to the top edge of Mount Grace Wood where, veering right, it drops through the trees and out into

cattle pasture. In the absence of an obvious trod, you make for the stream ahead, effectively the lower edge of a large field, which connects to Mount Lodge Farm near the Priory.

Built between 1397 and 1440, Mount Grace was Yorkshire's only Carthusian monastery. Monks lived here in solitude but in considerably more comfort than we normally associate with monastic life. Each had his own cell comprising study, bedroom, workroom and small garden, water being piped from hillside springs. Lay brothers apparently undertook the harder manual work, leaving the monks to their secluded life of books, gardening and prayer.

Abandoned after the Dissolution of the Monasteries in 1539, the buildings were exposed to stone theft and erosion by the elements, so that only the ground floor has survived. Nevertheless, Mount Grace remains one of Britain's best examples of a Carthusian foundation and is owned and cared for by the National Trust.

You've no alternative but to retrace steps back up to Chapel Wood Farm—the busy A19 constitutes a virtual no-go area to pedestrians! By forking right just north of the farm, an uphill field path will take you to a stand of pines sheltering the Lady Chapel, attached to a stone house. It was built around 1515, reputedly by Katherine of Aragon, first wife of Henry VIII, as a Chapel of Ease for Mount Grace Priory. A broad access track runs down south to join Rueberry Lane, curving round the flanks of Rueberry Hill. Beyond bungalows you meet Quarry Lane, where a right turn leads quickly back to Osmotherley's market cross.

WALK 6: *The Cleveland Escarpment — Osmotherley to Kildale*

Terrain: Well-walked paths and tracks but many steep gradients. Muddy after rain and exposed to rough weather. No refreshment points.
Start: Osmotherley's market cross. **Finish:** Kildale village. **Distance:** 19 miles (31km)—allow a full day—say, 10 hours. **Maps:** OS Landranger Sheets 99, 100, 93 and 94! Outdoor Leisure South-West and North-West sheets.

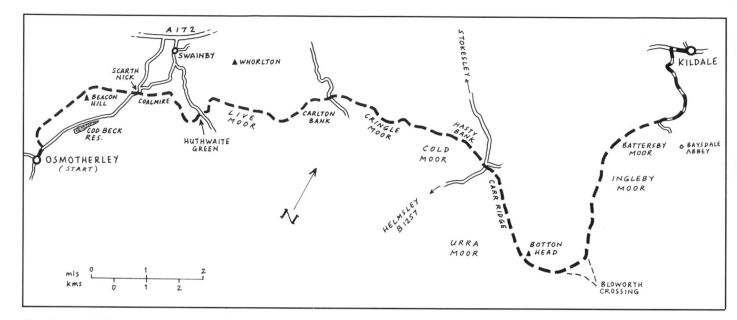

The Cleveland Hills escarpment is tramped by many feet. When you consider how close it lies to the conurbations of Middlesborough and Teesside, and that a traverse along its very edge is incorporated into so many well loved walks, little wonder the path is a broad one!

Following increased public interest in outdoor activities over the past decade, particularly walking, popular areas of Britain are, without question, suffering from over use. The Countryside Commission and National Park authorities, along with other voluntary bodies, do sterling work in repairing footpaths, but at the end of the day the sheer volume of human traffic across vulnerable terrain creates problems of erosion and litter which are difficult to solve in the long term.

Encouraging walkers to visit less frequented areas is a useful strategy, though thoughtful members of the walking fraternity have been doing just that for years! Unfortunately it is often the most beautiful and spectacular locations—landscape showpieces which everyone wants to see—that attract the greatest number of visitors and thus suffer the most serious consequences.

It will escape no-one's attention that the Cleveland Hills escarpment is one such location. There is fine, rough walking along its switchback crest and views out over the Cleveland Plain are airily magnificent. It has been adopted as part of such well known hikes as the Cleveland Way and the Lyke Wake Walk, among others, because it offers a walking experience unique to the North York Moors.

Previous page: **Looking back to Hasty Bank from Carr Ridge.**

Although eroded in places—you would be hard pressed to lose the way!—the terrain is generally firm and seems unlikely to incur the kind of extensive damage associated with, for example, boggy stretches of the Pennine Way, or steep fellsides in the Lake District. I have heard it argued that Land Rover tracks made for grouse shooting scar the moors more obtrusively than any number of walkers' paths, however well used.

This ambitious walk starts at Osmotherley because it is here that the Hambleton Hills, culminating in Black Hambleton (1309ft/399m), end and the scarp face of the Cleveland Hills begins its eastward run. Interrupted by the beginnings of Esk Dale (where we finish) and less well defined beyond Roseberry Topping, the escarpment continues towards the coast around Staithes.

I recommend an early start in favourable weather and carrying plentiful supplies of food and drink. Car owning friends could meet you at two points where roads cross gaps in the escarpment, and at Kildale unless accommodation has been arranged there.

Once a bustling market town, Osmotherley is now well visited by holidaymakers and walkers, though it retains a kind of sleepy, old-fashioned ambience. There is much excellent walking in the vicinity and a variety of accommodation too, including a camp site and youth hostel north of the village.

In fact, it is uphill towards the latter that we set off, turning left into residential Rueberry Lane. You will notice a carved Cleveland Way signpost, first of many on this hike which is coincident with that long-distance trail. At other points a simple acorn logo appears, symbol for all Britain's official long-distance paths.

The shoulder of Rueberry Hill provides marvellous, elevated views over Osmotherley, set on its natural shelf between moorland heights and the Vale of Mowbray. Chapel Farm, soon to be passed, has always struck me as especially picturesque. From it, one path (none too clear on the ground) leads down left to Mount Grace Priory, another up right to Lady's Chapel: both detours are unlikely to appeal on this occasion but are worth making, and covered in greater detail by Walk 5.

The often muddy cart track now skirts a wall alongside three fields, then you fork right into South Wood, open views replaced by the shady intimacy of mixed forest as height is steadily gained. Trees—mostly regenerated birch—thin towards the top of the escarpment and eyes will soon become fixed ahead upon an array of aerials and dishes sprouting from a British Telecom transmission booster station. Here on Beacon Hill, some 900ft (275m) above the Vale of Mowbray, fire beacons were lit to warn of invasion or to commemorate special events long before the age of telecommunications. Beyond the heads of sitka spruce clothing the scarp, you might spot the Pennines far to the west, but it is to the east that eyes should be focused, for there lies a succession of moorland humps terminating in the pronounced escarpment we are to follow.

For many years Beacon Hill's triangulation pillar at 981ft (299m) above sea level was the starting point for the 40-mile (64-km) Lyke Wake Walk, a challenging route across the moorland watershed to the coast at Ravenscar. Erosion and noise disturbance often accompany organised events involving groups of people and the start has been moved to Sheepwash car park down to the east.

Gates lead out to the open flanks of Scarth Wood Moor and a well blazed path through the heather. Gentle slopes at first steepen by a wall at the tarmac road in Scarth Nick, a notch in the escarpment created by glacial meltwater during the last Ice Age.

Across the road by a cattle grid, a wicket gate and a Lyke Wake Walk sign indicate the route forward on a forestry road through Coalmire Plantation, soon dropping abruptly into the pretty valley of Scugdale Beck. At a gated lane to Swainby, you swing right up the valley on a wide, wooded path below Limekiln Bank that used to take all prizes for the stickiest, deepest mud but has been tamed in recent years by deposits of stone chippings! In just over half a mile you take a well signed path left down pasture to a ford, then cross the road bridge over

Right: **The way into Coalmire Plantation at Scarth Nick.**

Below: **Views out over the Cleveland Plain are airily magnificent.**

Scugdale Beck which takes you up past Hollin Hill Farm to the little crossroads at Huthwaite Green.

Ironstone mining on the flanks of Whorlton Moor and in Scugdale during the latter half of the nineteenth century has given way to forestry, an altogether more peaceful industry which, nonetheless, has transformed much of the northern escarpment. The dale sides were also worked for jet, and old spoil heaps line the 900ft (300m) contour like gargantuan molehills.

Huthwaite Green, the tiniest of hamlets on a back road south-east of Swainby, represents the beginning of true moorland for the escarpment walker. Ahead lies an exciting switchback of summits which does not relent until Urra Moor is reached, 9 miles (14km) distant.

To the right of a telephone kiosk a track climbs past overgrown ironstone mine spoil towards Live Moor Plantation fence and swings left onto a bridleway to Faceby. In a few hundred metres, waymarked unequivocally, the path turns up a plantation firebreak and its long flight of steps (an improvement on the former muddy scramble!) is guaranteed to get heart and lungs working, no matter how fit you are!

A stile marks the boundary of open ground on Live Moor where the gradient eases off, though you miss the highest point at 1033ft (315m) cairned to the south of the path. These days the path is well hollowed out—the result of countless trudging boots—and in wet weather can become quite slippery. Boundary stones and outcropping boulders of Ravenscar sandstone punctuate otherwise featureless moorland, but scarp slopes are always exhilarating places and eyes will be drawn to the north and east. Whorl Hill, a mere kilometre away, monopolises the foreground, while Roseberry Topping rears conically to the distant north-east.

Our track, a broad, pale motorway for walkers, can be seen rising over Carlton Moor, the next objective. Carlton Bank Gliding Club occupies the summit plateau; its runway, bulldozed level and stripped of heather, is out of bounds to walkers, but even adjacent moortop seems to have deteriorated into semi-desert. One Easter I found the ground here crazed with open cracks reminiscent of mudflats after a dry spell; the following year, rain had turned it into heavy, glutinous clay. In any event, the best going is along the rising escarpment edge where views are exceptionally fine.

Extensive alum workings on Carlton Bank below the trig. pillar and boundary stone at 1338ft (408m) closed in 1771. In recent years they have degenerated into a dusty (or muddy) wasteland beneath the onslaughts of scrambling bikes. The visual and audible pollution this causes is anathema to most walkers for whom the hills are a source of quiet inspiration. It is

only to be hoped that through sacrificing this location to that particularly intrusive sport, others will escape. On fine weekends, Carlton Bank is not a place to linger at, unless you relish becoming a spectator! Gliding, hang-gliding, mountain-biking, kite flying and walking, as well as motorcycle scrambling, are all likely to be taking place!

It may be with some relief that you cross the road linking Bilsdale with the Cleveland Plain and tackle the climb to Cringle End. At the top you will find a stone bench and a topograph—or view indicator—dedicated to Alec Falconer, champion of walkers' interests who died in 1968 aged 84.

The way veers right now, in a big concave sweep above precipitous crags, some way north from the actual summit at 1417ft (432m). Below, as if seen from a low-flying aircraft, farmland spreads out towards the distant urban sprawl of Middlesborough. Nearer to hand, an old track skirts the lower slopes where miners searched for jet during the last century. As a raw material from which ornaments and jewellery were fashioned it was in great demand, but finding deposits in the hillsides was often a hit and miss affair.

A depression with walled enclosures separates Cringle Moor from Cold Moor—another dome of land attained not without legwork and carpeted with bilberry and heather. Grouse are much in evidence, though the immediate escarpment edge is not used for shooting. Birds frequently wait until the very last moment before taking flight in a clatter of feathers and frantic squawks. I have never been able to fathom the psychology of this and reason it must stem either from rank laziness—a wistful hope that the approaching walker might, after all, change direction—or from immobilising fear leading to outright panic! A third possibility, sheer stupidity, does, however, spring more readily to mind!

By now, a pattern of ascent and descent is firmly established and with it, perhaps, the realisation that the route is a tough one! Spare a thought, however, for long-distance backpackers carrying bulky gear, especially those who are lightweight camping, and your own modest day pack will seem a little lighter!

Taking a gate into a field and following the obvious path, you work your way upwards above Broughton Plantations into a miniature rock landscape. The Wainstones' pinnacles and blocks are popular with climbers of all abilities and even the walking route involves an entertaining scramble. Above, on Hasty Bank, there are tremendous views down the escarpment cliffs towards Clay Bank Top and its conspicuous car park.

Compared to preceding descents, the ensuing one is lengthier. Reaching the B1257 be-

tween Stokesley and Helmsley represents an important turning point in this itinerary. Only one more significant ascent remains, but you pass no other human habitation or road for the next 6 miles (9.5km) or so: if a towel is to be thrown in, this is the place to do it! I wouldn't call what follows remote in a wilderness sense—farms on the plain are never more than a mile or two away as the crow flies. However, the big, afforested escarpment prevents an easy retreat should weather or circumstances deteriorate. In thick mist you need to keep checks on your position to avoid taking the wrong track in a couple of places (possibly confirming direction by compass) but for the most part, route finding is perfectly straightforward.

Directly across the road from the steps just descended, a gate leads you up by a forest boundary wall and over grassy hillside. Above a stile there are rocks to contend with and the muddy path shows signs of heavy wear in this accessible and popular spot; you are soon levelling off onto the peaty crest of Carr Ridge. A great sense of freedom and openness accompanies walks on these moortops, yet there is little of specific visual interest other than boundary stones and the occasional grouse. According to disposition, you either concentrate on making rapid progress or allow the mind to wander on a higher plane! Before losing sight of it, glance back at the striking profile of Hasty Bank, surely the most impressive of the Cleveland Hills.

Urra Moor rises ahead and the track with it to Botton Head (or Round Hill), where a tumulus crowned with an OS triangulation pillar marks the Cleveland Hills' highest point, 1490ft (454m) above sea level. Looking back, the moorland summits already traversed peep above a foreground expanse of heather.

The Hand Stone and other inscribed stones are encountered as the 'highway' (which it once was) continues its easterly course, up to 20ft (6m) wide in places. I vividly recall a morning here, mist blowing over a watery sun and the acrid smell of charcoal rising from acres of burnt heather. It is burned systematically to encourage the growth of young shoots upon which grouse and sheep feed, and sometimes as a firebreak.

At Cockayne Head, the old road begins to dip and veer right towards Bloworth Crossing. During the nineteenth century, trains carrying iron-ore crossed the moors from mines around Rosedale and were lowered by cable down the escarpment at Ingleby Incline. From there they joined the main rail network to the smelting mills of Teesside and Durham. Bloworth Crossing, where the old coaching road along Rudland Rigg crossed the railway, was permanently manned but is now just an intersection of ways. The railway's cinder trackbed is much travelled by hikers.

Walkers admiring the view north from the summit of Carlton Bank — 1338ft (408m) above sea level.

You can visit Bloworth Crossing then turn back sharp left along the stony moor road, though there is a short-cut path north-east through the heather past shooting butts and over the old railway trackbed, emerging on the rough road by the remains of a moorland cross inscribed 1888. The way has swung round to west of north across the watershed between Bransdale and Farndale to the south and the Cleveland Plain to the north.

Before summer warmth has teased greenery from the earth, surrounding moor grasses are pale and tawny, their colour leached out by winter cold and a dearth of sunlight. From mid-August onwards, you are walking through a landscape turned acid-purple from the flowers of heather and ling.

It is plain going on a stony swath along the escarpment edge. From Tidy Brown Hill on Ingleby Moor, you start losing height and within $1\frac{1}{2}$ miles (2.5km) the narrow tarmac road on Battersby Moor is reached. It ends at Baysdale Farm down to the right but our interest in it lies ahead

for, beyond a cattle grid, altitude is quickly lost and a farewell bade to the escarpment.

The walk, however, is not quite over. Views west are as extensive as ever and with virtually no traffic to bother you there is ample time to savour them before the gated lane takes you round beneath The Park (a spur of Kildale Moor) and onto the Esk valley road. Kildale village, a few hundred metres to the right, possesses a friendly Post Office and General Store, but you will be lucky to arrive before it closes!

Great Hograh Moor (top left) from the path below Kildale Moor.

WALK 7: *Baysdale and Kildale Moors*

Terrain: A moor road, then rough moorland paths, poorly defined in places; clear paths and tracks to end with. Numerous ascents and descents over rugged ground. **Start/Finish:** Kildale village. **Distance:** 14 miles (23km)—allow 6 to 7 hours. **Maps:** OS Landranger Sheet 94; Outdoor Leisure North-West sheet.

This is one of those walks best kept for a fine day. Only masochists enjoy tramping over wild, rough country in mist and rain, though admittedly there is nothing like it for sharpening map and compass skills! One of the route's great joys is the succession of wide-ranging views it provides you with—there is no better way to get acquainted with these northernmost Cleveland Hills than to witness their slowly changing perspectives as you complete the circular tour.

It is a longish hike with no refreshment points along the way, so a rucksack stocked with food, drink and energy rations will add to your enjoyment and safety. Being somewhat off the beaten track compared to many other classic walks in the region, and with no real escape route in the lonelier middle section, the outing deserves to be taken moderately seriously: sensible precautions would be obtaining a weather forecast and letting a responsible person know your plans for the day.

Kildale lies at the western end of Esk Dale, that major east-west valley completely dissecting the National Park. Its upper waters, in particular Lonsdale Beck and the River Leven, flow unexpectedly west and there is a shallow pass between Kildale and Commondale before the Esk establishes its easterly course towards the North Sea at Whitby. Food and drink to take with you are available at Kildale's little Post Office/General Store, while along by the railway station (on the scenic Esk Valley line), near the restored church, is the site of Kildale Castle. It was abandoned way back in Tudor times and even the motte has been occupied by a modern farmstead, so there is little for the untrained eye to see.

Most walkers—myself included—prefer naturally uneven ground to tarmac and a preliminary glance at the map will reveal a couple of miles of road walking to begin this route. However, there is road walking and road walking! Sharing your way with a constant stream of traffic, especially without a pavement or verge, is unpleasant in the extreme and accounts for far more injuries and fatalities than incidents 'on the hill'. But on minor roads carrying just the infrequent vehicle— and this is one of them—walking can be perfectly enjoyable: with no cause to watch every footfall, attention is freed to admire the surroundings.

Once you have left the Easby road 500m west of Kildale and turned left towards the moors, you are on a gated, cul-de-sac lane whose tarmac ends at Baysdale Farm below Battersby Moor. It is *en route* for nowhere else, so, apart from the occasional fellow walker and the odd passing farm vehicle, you will have it all to yourself.

Climbing doesn't begin in earnest until you have drawn beneath a crag called The Park, the

western bastion of Kildale Moor. From there on, past a disused quarry and accompanied by ever widening vistas over the Cleveland Plain in good visibility, steady effort is required to gain over 300ft (100m) of height.

Levelling off at a right-hand bend on Warren Moor, you are no more than 500m from the River Leven's source over to the east. Back north runs Park Dyke, one of several groups of ancient earthworks near western escarpments in the National Park, some of which extend in excess of a mile. Best known, perhaps, are the Scamridge Dykes near the south-eastern edge of Dalby Forest between Pickering and Scarborough. Unlike most other antiquities of this kind, dykes seem to have eluded conclusive dating and some, it is thought, may have been constructed as late as the Middle Ages.

The moortop attained, eyes must be peeled to spot a stout wooden post on the right about 250m beyond the second gate. Opposite it, a feint trod strikes off left through the heather; it soon grows in confidence, passes through a wall gap by a tree and follows a field wall down to the road-end at Baysdale Farm, having thus saved you a kilometre of tarmac tramping by short-cutting a long corner. Past the farm buildings, a surfaced track takes you on towards the squared, grey elevations of Baysdale Abbey.

No mellow, evocative ruin this, but a working farm and living accommodation. Keeping the road open in a bad winter must concentrate mind and body wonderfully, but what an idyllic location! Although only a few carved stones and a medieval ribbed bridge remain, this is the site of a twelfth-century Cistercian nunnery.

In deteriorating weather or in other pressing circumstances, two short-cut options present themselves here. Most drastic is to turn left on the track alongside Baysdale Beck, forking left across it about half a mile (800m) farther on. This way takes you past ruined barns and through fields on the flanks of Kildale Moor to join the main route's return leg at Map Ref: 633 078. Less extreme would be to omit the big loop round Baysdale's headwaters (an altogether lonelier section) by climbing across two fields behind Baysdale Abbey and resuming the route at Thorntree house.

From a field corner gate directly in front of the large house, you set off south-west up over pasture to a gap between fence and wall. Mounting the lower slopes of Middle Head, you slant half-right up to a gate and stile, then fork right on a clear track up through bracken and a threadbare plantation. Here, a gate in the intake wall gives onto open moor.

Keeping to the right ensures a line over good springy turf along Middle Head above the afforested valley of Grain Beck. About 2 miles (3km) from Baysdale Abbey, having encountered

a row of grouse butts on more level terrain, you reach a path junction. Trods west and north-west cross Ingleby Moor to the escarpment—$\frac{3}{4}$ mile (1.2km) away as the grouse flies—along which runs a broad, stony track used by shooting parties and long-distance walkers on the Cleveland Way and other routes. So, as you continue ahead down over increasingly wet and reedy ground on the old 'Flagged Road' track (remnants of a paved causeway), feelings of remoteness from civilisation must be tempered by the knowledge that farms on the plain below Greenhow Bank are relatively close at hand, though not easy to get to!

Armouth Wath is a derelict sheepfold situated where streams draining the surrounding bowl of moorland converge into Grain Beck and thence into Baysdale itself. Bridgestones span Black Hagg Beck where the trees peter out, and a rising path past more butts heads off east, steepish to begin with then easing and swinging north on Stockdale Moor. In fact, you are following the watershed between upper Baysdale and upper Westerdale over indeterminate moorland, so your direction—a little east of north—is best confirmed by compass if in any doubt.

In under a mile, a clearer track will have been joined at a pile of stones; it takes you east of higher ground on Nicholas Ruck and meets a well used, stony jeep track. Walking left along it, sweeping views stretch to all horizons, with Roseberry Topping and Captain Cook's Monument conspicuous to the north-west. Half a mile along the gently descending track, a thin path branches left in a shallow groove to the corner of a wire fence and thence down to the plantation edge where a right turn brings you along to a gate. If the path is missed, you will leave rights-of-way as such, though the jeep track could be followed down to the same plantation gate.

Just before reaching Thorntree House below, the route turns right, skirting two fields below rampant bracken alive with young grouse in early summer. Wall stile and gate lead down and up to The Low House (or Shepherds House on some maps), across a lawn—apparently the correct way despite sensations of invading privacy—and on up a forestry track to the open flanks of Holiday Hill.

With recent intricacies of route-finding now largely behind us, the way trends progressively southwards and forks off left towards the top end of a tree belt in Great Hograh Beck. On a sunny day you could hardly wish for a more agreeable picnic spot. The miniature stone bridge paved with slabs and inscribed 1938 belongs in fact to a much older packhorse way known as Skinner Howe Cross Road, though at hardly a boot's width its declining use has reduced it to a skimpy path. Over the beck you bear half-left after 50m, walking east now over heather and bracken past a scattering of large rocks and enigmatic standing stones on the north facing slopes of Great Hograh Moor.

During late August the moors around Baysdale, in common with many other locations in the National Park, undergo a stunning intensification of colour as heather and ling come into flower. Hillside swathes of acid purple produce technicolour contrasts with bracken, whose fronds, still vibrant green at their base, take on early-autumn yellow and orange and russet brown. If you are blessed with fine weather at this time, walking becomes a continuous visual feast!

In due course Little Hograh Beck is crossed—no more than a tuck in the moorside blanket—and the path arrives at John Breckon Road. In recent years this has been surfaced, presumably to facilitate access to farms in Upper Westerdale. Four hundred metres along to the left lies the Westerdale to Kildale road and at the bottom of the hill there is both ford and footbridge, the latter indispensable when Baysdale Beck is in spate! At other times, plentiful parking on grassy, beckside levels attracts picnickers to this delightful spot—a good one from which to contemplate Baysdale's unusual wildness and beauty. No motor road penetrates west of this point, the few inhabitants from areas already explored by this walk relying on the narrow road over Battersby Moor to reach Kildale.

Just 300m up the Kildale road, a wide path leaves to the left through bracken, dipping and rising along Kildale Moor and yielding definitive views of Baysdale. At a derelict building you leave the boundary wall, striking up right off its corner and threading through heather and the ubiquitous bracken in a generally north-west direction. Over the crest of Kildale Moor, the path heads downhill past land drainage channels to a small conifer plantation in Leven Vale. Though the River Leven appears to flow east towards Esk Dale and the coast, it swings west above Kildale and out across the Cleveland Plain through Stokesley.

All that now remains of the outing is to savour the last elevated views, both behind and ahead towards Commondale Moor. With a mile left to walk, you climb to Warren Farm and take the farm road west down through Little Kildale Wood. Where Green Gate Lane meets the Commondale road, a left turn brings you quickly back to Kildale village.

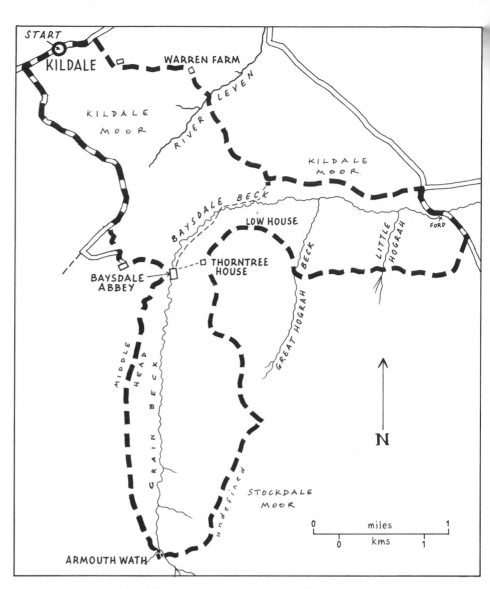

Right: **A reminder of winter above Baysdale Farm.**

Facing page: **Captain Cook's Monument.**

WALK 8: *Highcliffe Nab, Roseberry Topping and Captain Cook's Monument*

Terrain: Good tracks and paths over undulating heather moorland with one steep ascent. **Start/Finish:** Lonsdale Plantation, Kildale Moor. **Distance:** 9½ miles (15.5km)—allow 4 to 5 hours. **Maps:** OS Landranger Sheet 93; Outdoor Leisure North-West sheet.

Two distinctive features in the north-western landscape of the National Park stand sufficiently close together to form the fulcrum around which this fine upland hike revolves. Roseberry Topping's broken conical summit, ravaged by mining and landslip, rears unmistakeably from the Cleveland Plain. Its profile—an anomalous shark's fin on otherwise rolling horizons—can be identified from many miles away in clear visibility. Two miles (4km) south-east on Easby Moor and a place of pilgrimage for followers of the legendary, local-born navigator and explorer, stands the monument to Captain Cook. Conspicuous like Roseberry Topping, it, too, offers views par excellence over the Cleveland escarpment and west to the Pennines.

A gated moor lane leaves the Kildale to Commondale road 1½ miles (2.4km) east of Kildale village at the top of Percy Rigg. It crosses Brown Hill and runs alongside Lonsdale Plantation, delivering you to the conjunction of several moorland tracks; there is limited parking space at the road end or on verges. You begin by walking south-east back along the ribbon of tarmac, remembering perhaps the Scottish engineer John McAdam whose road surfacing invention allows our cars to speed us across hitherto rough and time-consuming terrain for better or for worse!

In about half a mile (800m), you turn left on a 'Private Road to Sleddale' which excludes motorists but not walkers and takes you out over heather moor. After zig-zagging down over Sleddale Slack, you reach the final bend leading towards Sleddale Farm and here swing left up a clear track climbing the gentle eastern flanks of Codhill Heights. Directly ahead, the low, dark edge of forest is broken and it is towards this hiatus that the walk aims, soon forking left onto a grassier track and heading for a clump of tall deciduous trees. You will find a handgate in a wall corner—the key to a 400m detour to Highcliff Nab, reached by forking right in the woods; you will be treading the Cleveland Way path, a much used thoroughfare and very clear on the ground. From the craggy outcrop there are good views north over Guisborough and beyond to the Tees.

Retracing steps to the handgate, you now turn right down by a wall. Beyond Highcliffe Farm the going gets distinctly squelchy but at a sheep dip in a wall corner you bear left to cross The Race by plank bridge and climb through bracken onto the firm shoulder of Black Nab. Countless boots along the Cleveland Way have etched through the thin moorland topsoil, here just as elsewhere along its meandering loop from Helmsley to the coast. All long-distance footpaths eventually suffer similar fates and it is hard to foresee an improvement when trends suggest ever increasing interest in walking and other outdoor activities, coupled with greater leisure time.

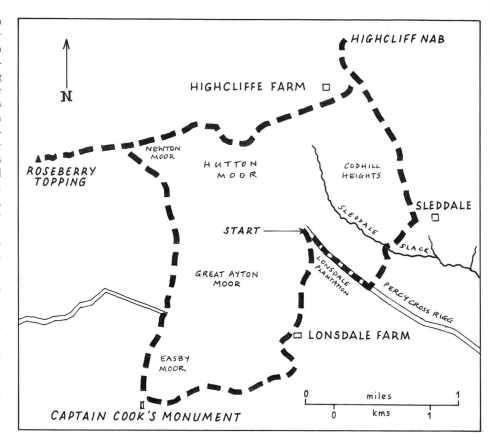

Veering right onto a broader track on Hutton Moor, you are less than a mile from Lonsdale Plantation—a useful short-cut if time or conditions are pressing. A left turn at the forest edge (either, it seems, outside or inside the fence there) brings you along to a corner in the plantation, a cue to bear left through a gate by a post and to walk up over the diminutive but strategic Newton Moor: strategic because, cresting a rise, a dramatic view unfolds. Before you rises the smoothed-off pyramid of Roseberry Topping, while farther south Captain Cook's Monument is interposed against the blue rim of the Cleveland Hills' northern escarpment.

As ascent of Roseberry Topping is technically 'off route' and if onward progress is of the essence, then the hill can simply be admired from afar and left for another day. However, I do recommend a sortie to its 1050ft (320m) summit: from your present position, the climb, after an initial modest descent, is only 266ft (81m)—compared to a beefier 750ft (215m) from the car park at Newton-under-Roseberry. Unless you reach the top, you may find it hard to believe that the west face is all crag and rock and that in mist or gale the precipitous edge can be dangerous. If you arrive in good visibility, airy panoramas amply reward the leg work involved in getting up.

Roseberry Topping is a singular hill, a strange hybrid formed by natural forces and the hand of man. Originally an island of rock protruding from a glacier's surface during the last Ice Age (such features are called 'nunataks' or 'rognons'), its geology is unstable and occasional rock falls continue to modify its profile. Until the seventeenth century, the hill was known as 'Osbury Toppyne' and fire beacons lit upon its summit warned of the Spanish Armada and later of Charles Stuart's rebellious Jacobites. In more recent times, quarrying for jet, iron-ore and roadstone exacerbated erosion—although overgrown, some of the old workings are still discernible.

Situated so close to centres of population, an exciting landmark such as this attracts considerable attention from bona fide walkers and climbers as well as from less responsible people for whom the 'mountain' is eminently accessible. Once acquired by the National Trust, an appeal was launched to finance much-needed work on paths, fences, woodland and bracken control and at my last visit a paved pathway lower down the west side seemed to have established a normal ascent route, though graffiti continues to deface the summit OS pillar.

Down to the south-west, the village of Great Ayton is where James Cook went to school, while due south stands Airy Holme Farm where he spent part of his boyhood—but more of that later! Back at the gate on Newton Moor, our itinerary turns right beside the wall above Slacks Wood, then contours along the western lip of Great Ayton Moor. Hut circles, cairns and ancient earthworks—best seen after heather burning—provide visible links with our prehistoric ancestors who settled here in a climate much kinder than our own. Within a mile you descend eroded hillside to a car parking and picnic area at the end of a lane rising from Great Ayton and pass through a gate almost opposite. The wide, stony track between trees leads steadily uphill and ends in steps onto Easby Moor top. Robert Campion, a Whitby financier, erected the 51ft (15.5m) monument to Captain Cook in 1828, the centenary of his birth. The great circumnavigator's story is all there on cast-iron plaques, though the language used is dated.

Born in 1728 on the outskirts of Middlesbrough, son of a Scottish farm labourer and his Yorkshire wife, James Cook attended school in Great Ayton after the family had moved to Airy Holme Farm in 1736. After a few years as farm hand he eventually left home, aged 14, to work as an apprentice draper in Staithes. He did not stay long! Already passionately interested in the sea, he served 9 years in North Sea colliers before entering the Royal Navy at 27, progressing rapidly through the ranks and joining expeditions to the then new lands of Canada and Newfoundland. So great had his reputation as a navigator become by the mid-1700s that he commanded surveys of New Zealand and the east Australian coast in HMS *Endeavour* and went on to chart the South Pacific. On February 14th 1779, during a voyage to discover a new trading route to the East Indies, he was killed rescuing members of his crew from natives in Hawaii, where the expedition had put in for supplies.

There is a small museum in Great Ayton's schoolroom where Cook's interest in navigational mathematics was fired, and more material in Pannett Park Library, Whitby.

At 1063ft (324m) above sea level, you are higher than Roseberry Topping yet there is little sense of a summit on this wooded plateau. Views, however, are no less expansive and the escarpment edge here is dramatically rocky. Turning east from the monument, still for the time being on the Cleveland Way path, you approach a plantation corner, pass through a wall and fence gate and walk in larch forest, more or less on the level. Offshoot tracks to left and right are ignored as you proceed east on a surfaced roadway to a gate where the Cleveland Way turns abruptly right down towards Kildale.

The concluding stage of this walk turns left past mature conifers, downhill and swinging right to emerge again into open country past Lonsdale Farm. Once over the beck, the farm road veers left at a cluster of barns, but you keep straight ahead through a gate and up a stony track. At first it mounts Nab End along the boundary of Lonsdale Plantation but soon ducks into the trees and deposits you nicely back at the road end on Percy Cross Rigg.

Roseberry Topping from the path on Newton Moor.

Above: **The ever-popular summit of Roseberry Topping and . . .**

Far left: **. . . the view west across the Cleveland Plain.**

Left: **The distant Cleveland Hills escarpment from Easby Moor.**

Facing page: **Hob on the Hill — as far from the madding crowd as you can get!**

WALK 9: *Commondale, Hob on the Hill and Quakers' Causeway*

Terrain: Moorland paths and tracks, some parts undefined; a little road walking. Exposed in bad weather. **Start/Finish:** Commondale village. **Distance:** 7 miles (11km). **Maps:** OS Landranger Sheet 94; Outdoor Leisure North-West sheet.

Situated at the crossing of many ancient tracks, Commondale is a fine walking centre. Unless you stay down in the dale bottom, however (there are good walks along to Castleton and Danby), you will need to go prepared for potentially tough outings, particularly if the weather is blustery. Much of the charm of Commondale Moor lies in the quality of distant views embracing high ground from as far afield as Bilsdale Moor in the south-west to the moors above Rosedale in the south-east and the coast around Skinningrove and Staithes. There are a few steep gradients but the landscape's scale is deceptive and paths indistinct, especially in the walk's middle section: not a place for misty days unless you can navigate expertly using map and compass!

Commondale village stands at the confluence of Ravengill and Whiteley becks and the Cleveland Inn will satisfy appetites and thirsts at the end of a walk! You begin by heading up the road towards Kildale, past the Commondale roadside sign to a pull-in by a conspicuous stand of Scots pines. A hundred metres or so along the stony track ahead you cut across over grass to the right on a signposted footpath to Guisborough; very quickly you come upon a section of paved causeway leading to marshy ground by North Ings Slack.

Paved packhorse ways, though not unique to the North York Moors, are exceptionally common here: only in the South Pennines does a network of comparable size exist. Increasingly boggy conditions brought about by a wetter, cooler period in our climate during the fourteenth century made communications and the transportation of goods between abbeys and farms difficult. Certainly some paved ways date back to these early monastic times, but it was the emergence of industries such as coal and ironstone mining, charcoal burning, spinning, weaving and lime-burning that created a demand for year-round, all-weather tracks. Without firm footing, laden ponies would soon get bogged down in mud and marsh.

Waggons were of limited use over rough upland terrain and could carry far less than a train of 30 or 40 pack ponies. Conventional cart traffic combined with water erosion often turned lanes into sunken channels, so the causeway builders laid their sandstone slabs along the raised side banks. Most commodities would have been moved by packhorse before the arrival of railway transport in the mid-nineteenth century and it is thought that the 150 miles (240km) of causeway traceable in the region represents a mere fraction of the original complex network.

As maps reveal, there are Monks' Ways, Quakers' Paths, Smugglers' Paths, Panniermens' Tracks, Church Ways and Mill Ways, many partly buried beneath more modern roads and tracks. Individual stone slabs have become hollowed by centuries-long use and it is this tangible connection between our own footsteps and those of people living several hundred years ago that endows causeways with special fascination.

Short though it may be, you have just walked a good section of paved way, including an excellent example of a Bridgestone over Whiteley Beck; parallel slabs like these are less usual than a single slab.

Our path continues up the bracken and heather clad flanks of Skelderskew Moor, leaving the little valley and bringing you adjacent to North Ings Farm with its geometric plantation. There are grouse butts up to the right and eventually the path gives out onto a stony jeep track at a plank bridge. If you care to, fork left to look at the simple memorial stone down to your left: Guardsmen Alf Cockerill and Robbie Leggott, both victims of World War I, spent their boyhood on these moors.

At my last visit, a green cabin had been installed at the trackside a little farther ahead, presumably for use by intrepid shooting parties. Whether or not you approve of grouse shooting, it continues to play a significant part in moorland management. The birds, I'm afraid, have my sympathy and I would welcome an end to their senseless killing in the name of 'sport'. Bulldozed tracks, sometimes obliterating footpaths and bridleways, provide access for convoys of 4-wheel-drive vehicles after the 'Glorious Twelfth', but in the process do more to deface the moorland environment than all your walkers put together. Should you be unlucky enough to encounter a shoot while out on a hike, you have the unenviable choice of either waiting until it is over or finding somewhere else to walk!

As you climb gradually higher, views open out all round across a landscape in which the only punctuation marks are grouse butts and pale jumbles of rock. When the track levels out and trends left, it is time to strike off to the right on a heathery trod of sorts, a little west of north. Still walking perceptibly uphill, you need to aim right of two grouse butts; by the time the path (really no more than flattened heather) gives up the ghost, the low mound and stone pillar inscribed 'Hob on the Hill' should be visible.

Part of a paved packhorse way near the start at Commondale.

The path down to Commondale from the moor road corner.

The dales are, of course, very beautiful, but for me the landscapes of Commondale Moor and others like it epitomise the great attraction of this National Park: sweeping panoramas, unenclosed space, clean air and an absence of crowds. How often have I tramped the high moors and met not another soul! I imagine these lonely wildernesses of heather rolling from horizon to horizon are not everyone's cup of tea, yet they offer a brand of spirit-lifting freedom that lovers of solitude and distance cannot resist.

Unless you are being blown off your feet, Hob on the Hill is a marvellous place to savour. Hobs, incidentally, cousins to elves and goblins, belong to that dim half-world of spells and superstition, of magic and curses. Some 24 hobs are associated with locations in the North York Moors and, with a few mischievous exceptions, seem to have been helpful creatures, curing illness or protecting crops.

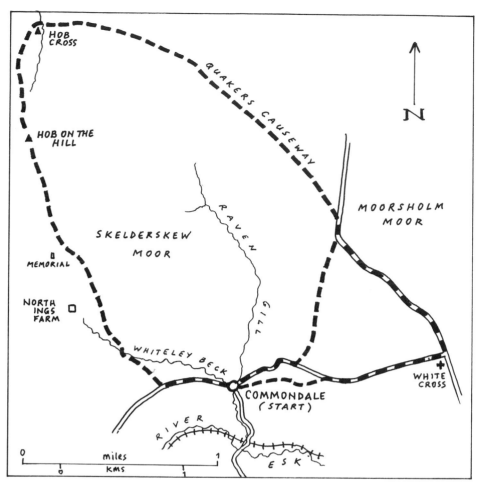

If the weather is closing in, you are only 300m north-east of the jeep track, but in poor visibility the onward route needs careful navigation. Hob Cross is your next objective—three-quarters of a mile (1.2km) downhill on a bearing a smidgin west of north in the shallow valley of Tidkinhow Slack. Hob Cross, another inscribed pillar, stands within a stone's throw of Tidkinhow Farm's intake wall, parallel to which you turn east on a narrow track marked with blue-arrowed posts. Half a mile or so after passing beneath overhead wires you join the Quakers' Path above Lockwood Beck Reservoir. Turning right, you will discover another clearly exposed length of paved causeway; it doesn't last all the way to the Smeathorns Road connecting Castleton and Commondale with the busy A171, but there are several tumuli to look out for on the ensuing level mile.

No more than 100m of tarmac need be trodden, for off the road bend a thinnish path heads south towards Commondale. Before turning your back on the tops, a last 360 degree twirl is worth making. The sea is still visible beyond roadside snow stakes on Moorsholm Moor, while due west across the intervening valley of Raven Gill lies the unmistakeable hard-edged block of North Ings Plantation. The way back is uncomplicated: by keeping left of the wood, you reach the road at Sand Hill and walk down past Commondale's red-brick chapel to the Cleveland Inn.

The recommended conclusion to this hike (adding a little distance) is to continue along the unfenced moor road to a junction where you will find the base and shaft of White Cross. Here the old west road from Whitby may have divided, one arm heading for Stokesley, the other to Guisborough on Quakers' Causeway. In any event, experts consider both shaft and base of White Cross to be 'modern'; the upper section of the original cross can be seen in Whitby Museum.

It is all downhill now, first on the motor road, straight as a dye, then off the first bend by paved way, forking right towards the village. Here and there slabs are missing or grass covered, but two fields widths see you safely back at the village centre.

Left: **The roadside remains of White Cross above Commondale.**

Facing page: **A waymark post above Esklets in Upper Westerdale.**

WALK 10: *Upper Westerdale, Blakey Ridge and the Ironstone Railway*

Terrain: Rough valley and moor paths (one section undefined), a moor road and a disused railway trackbed. **Start/Finish:** Road end, Upper Westerdale. **Distance:** 8½ miles (13.5km)—allow 4 to 5 hours. **Maps:** OS Landranger Sheet 94; Outdoor Leisure North-West and South-West sheets.

Despite its modest length, this walk traverses a surprising variety of terrain. It takes you right into the heart of the moorland block separating those north-facing dales such as Westerdale and Danby Dale from their south-facing counterparts Farndale and Rosedale. Parts of the route are well frequented, at least during the summer, and the Lion Inn's presence on Blakey Ridge at the half-way point adds considerably to the attractiveness of the outing. Nevertheless, there is rugged terrain to contend with and a moderate amount of climbing, so hillwalking gear is called for. The final leg crosses trackless heather and in case of deteriorating weather a map and compass should be carried.

In contrast to Farndale which stretches 7 or 8 miles (12km) south to the Vale of Pickering, Westerdale twists narrowly into adjacent high ground. Farms here were virtually isolated until the road to Castleton was made up some 45 years ago, and it is near one of these—Waites House Farm—that you start out, taking care not to park in such a way that farm traffic is obstructed.

From the road end you turn left towards Waites House Farm, then immediately right on a surfaced lane to where footbridge and ford cross the infant Esk. Instead of crossing too, you strike off left onto a rather muddy path along the stream's east bank, signposted 'Footpath to Farndale'. Mounds of waste on The Nab above High House Farm over to the right date from the late nineteenth century when miners sought the then fashionable jet from which ornaments and jewellery were fashioned. Passing a stile and a gate you begin to gain a little height over often boggy ground, now heavily colonised by bracken where once stretched usable pasture.

Bracken is encountered on many of these classic walks and poses a real threat to moorside vegetation in the National Park. Spreading rapidly, it chokes the heather whose tender young shoots are eaten by sheep and grouse. New farming practices over the past half-century have led to the neglect of upland fields, allowing bracken a stranglehold from which escape is impossible without the widespread use of herbicides or radical changes in land use. Neither solution seems likely or even acceptable to an environment-conscious society. Yet bracken itself is obstructive to walkers and animals alike and recent studies suggest its spores may be harmful. Like rhododendrons, it quickly becomes an uncontrollable weed wherever it gains a foothold: in a few decades' time the moors may take on a different appearance beneath its tough, green mantle. Such a transition may seem 'unnatural', but we should remember that heather covered moorland derives from changes in our climate and centuries of exploitation by man during which the original broadleaved forests were depleted.

A good footbridge takes you to the Esk's west bank, still marshy from feeder streams, and past two fields and a shelter belt of Scots Pines. Walls are broken down and Esklets farmstead, a monastic grange of Rievaulx Abbey in the twelfth century, is now a total ruin. Until the mid-1940s the farm was still occupied, supplies having to be hauled over from the Castleton road by sled along the very path we are to follow. As this century has unfolded, lack of motor access and the absence of modern amenities have sounded the death knell of so many upland farmsteads in Britain. Once abandoned, even sturdy stone buildings soon succumb to the elements and the inexorable march of vegetation.

You walk right through Esklets and up the track over a tributary stream, forsaking the plain way climbing right and branching left instead across a field to a stand of trees. Keeping left of a reedy area, our now clearly visible path trends south-east to cross the headwaters of the Esk for positively the last time! Wall gaps follow and at a white-tipped post you turn left up a field edge. At the next post (old Lyke Wake markers) you veer right, heading for more wall gaps ahead and aided by the occasional white painted arrow on rocks.

A mile wide, Westerdale head marks the birthplace of the River Esk. From streamlets, springs and seepages draining the surrounding moors, this watercourse rapidly swells on its journey north and east to the North Sea at Whitby, 30 miles (48km) away.

Soon the old moorland path grows rougher but is never in doubt. With more determination now, freed from the valley's constraints, it climbs out past Esklets Crag and in another big step over High Hill Top provides the very best kind of rugged walking. You cross what remains of the intake wall and continue eastwards on an improving trod through the heather past grouse butts, eventually reaching the Margery Bradley stone beside the Castleton road above Rosedale Head.

Left: **A pathside grouse-butt on the moors above Esklets, Westerdale in the distance.**

Facing page: **At the Margery Bradley Stone.**

Rows of upright stones join with ancient crosses and tumuli to punctuate otherwise featureless expanses of moorland on the high plateaux. Boundary stones marking the perimeter of parishes and privately owned estates often bear carved initials denoting either the landowner's name (such as T.D. for Thomas Darley on Blakey Ridge, the Spaunton Manor boundary), or that of adjoining parishes ('R' for Rosedale, 'D' for Danby etc). A few rough old stones have acquired names and Margery Bradley is one such.

Having reached 1378ft (420m) at the northern end of Blakey Ridge, a mile of southward striding along the Castleton to Hutton-le-Hole road is accompanied by good views east into the bowl of Upper Rosedale. A branch of the old ironstone railway wound round the dale head from East Mines near Thorgill to Blakey Junction and although subsidence has taken its toll of the trackbed, it still forms a splendid walkers' route. On your right the moortop is peppered with old coal workings.

Before long you will arrive at the Lion Inn. Once patronised by coal and ironstone miners and today by walkers, cyclists and motorists, it has always been a welcome refreshment stop on

these bleak moors: at 1325ft (403m) it is one of England's highest pubs. When the car park is full to bursting on a summer weekend, I cannot help but feel that the pub's true character is masked. Arrive here off season on a stormy day, wet, buffeted by the wind and hungry, and there is nothing to compare with an hour or two in its cosy interior! Behind the inn stands Blakey Howe (or Cockpit Hill), a Bronze-age burial mound whose central hollow left by early grave robbers was reputedly used for cock-fighting between the seventeenth and nineteenth centuries.

Just north of the inn buildings, our route turns west over lumpy ground and in less than 500m reaches the trackbed of the Rosedale Ironstone Railway. Frequently walked, it forms part of several long-distance itineraries, including Alfred Wainwright's Coast to Coast Walk (St Bees in Cumbria to Robin Hood's Bay) and the famous Lyke Wake Walk. Whilst on it, no navigation is required—you might as easily be a train on rails—but should you wish to leave it by one of the moorland paths, keeping tabs on your progress is essential, especially in mist.

Tramping the cinder trackbed is not to everyone's liking though as it snakes round the head

of Farndale there are wide views south and west over the dale's fields bounded by the long horizon of Rudland Rigg. More pertinent, perhaps, is to spare a thought for this extraordinary railway. Ironstone from mines around Rosedale, already roasted in kilns to drive off water and carbonic acid gas and to reduce its weight, was loaded into metal waggons and sent off across the moors from Blakey Junction, not far south of the Lion Inn. The line's sheer audacity bears witness to the industry's vigour during its heyday in the 1870s. Cunningly negotiating the heads of Farndale and Bransdale without recourse to bridge or tunnel, the railway ran a total distance of 14 miles (22.5km) above 1000ft (300m) via Bloworth Crossing to Ingleby Incline. Here the waggons were lowered down the escarpment by cable to join the main rail network at Battersby Junction and thence to the smelting mills of Teesside and Durham.

Weather conditions, as one can imagine, were often severe. Heavy snowfall wreaked havoc, frequently closing the line, bringing down telephone cables and generally making life uncomfortable for all involved in the mining and transportation operations. The winter of 1895 proved to be the worst in the railway's entire

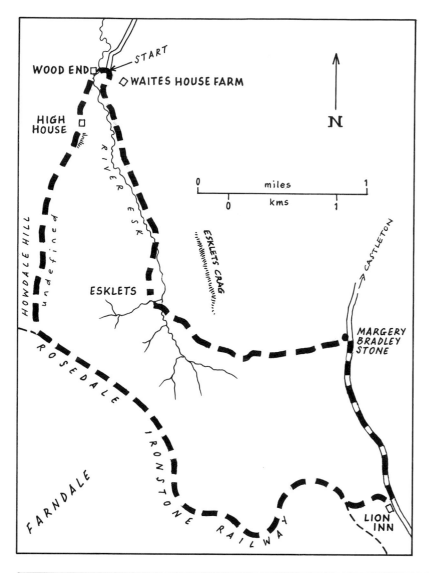

history, with huge snowdrifts blocking the line from January 2nd to mid-April and lingering in cuttings until mid-June. The hardships endured by railway employees and their families living in moor top cottages can scarcely have been equalled anywhere else in the country, yet, as is often the case in adversity, theirs was a friendly and happy community.

About 2 miles (3.2km) along the trackbed, you pass a sign on the right denoting the start of the Esk Valley Way: if needed, it provides a quick descent to Esklets and a return on the outward path. It is, however, always good to tread fresh ground throughout a walk and a mile further on, beyond a shallow cutting before the track curves left (Map Ref: 645 014), a thin path strikes off to the right, a little east of north. It gives up the ghost at some shooting butts but the way continues in the same direction over almost flat, trackless heather and bilberry.

By keeping east of Howdale Hill top and ascending only a modest amount, you will soon spot Waites House Farm ahead across Upper Westerdale. As the ground begins to fall, you cross patches of bog and stay just above rowan trees to the right of The Nab. A premature descent here could be dangerous, especially in poor visibility, as there is a line of crags below not depicted on maps.

A hundred metres or so beyond the rowans, you meet a clear track descending off the moor and crossing two fields to High House Farm. Ferocious barking dogs in the vicinity of the farmyard were chained up when I last passed by and I trust they will be similarly restrained in future! Below the gate, a metalled lane leads you over White Gill at a ford where you turn right to regain the dale road at Wood End.

Left: **The Lion Inn, Blakey — a welcome refreshment stop on the bleak moortops at 1325ft (403m).**

Facing page: **The unmistakable, slightly comical shape of Fat Betty on Danby High Moor.**

WALK 11: *Castleton, Fat Betty, Ralph Cross and Botton*

Terrain: Farm tracks, moorland paths (undefined in places) and high moor road. **Start/Finish:** Castleton. **Distance:** 12½ miles (20km)—allow about 6 hours. **Maps:** OS Landranger Sheet 94; Outdoor Leisure North-West Sheet.

Castleton is situated only a couple of miles west of Danby Moors Centre and is served by British Rail's Esk Valley line, though the station lies across the river at the dale bottom.

Castleton itself, rising on a spur of high land, owes its name to a timber-pallisaded castle put up atop an earth mound by Robert de Brus, head of the Lordship of Danby Forest, in 1089. Following William the Conqueror's incursion into Britain, his knights extended their command of country areas, harrying the north's Viking descendants in what amounted to a reign of terror. Although the castle stood for almost 130 years, its strategic importance never rivalled that of Scarborough and it was taken down in 1216; little remains except the banked motte, partly cut away by the modern motor road.

From the village centre, you set off on this wide-ranging hike by walking uphill, south-west past Moorlands Hotel. Where the main road swings left immediately beyond a right fork to Commondale, you keep straight ahead on a narrow, unfenced lane towards Westerdale. Already there are fine, unfolding views of this dale and of moorland slopes to the west.

When valley routes like this one thread across a matrix of fields and old tracks, the way needs careful following. The first key—a post box at a fork in the lane—leads you down a thin, grassy trod on the right through bracken and past a disused quarry to New Road, the main link between Castleton and Westerdale. You cross over and continue down to a gate, veering sharp left through more bracken to a footbridge over the infant River Esk.

A narrow path is now followed half-left, climbing pleasantly above a small wood and taking you out onto the rough, stony flanks of Westerdale Moor, clothed with bracken and bilberry. You soon pick up a clear track and shortly after passing a plantation of Scots pines on the left, cross a large stile and aim for a wall gap ahead, helped by the odd yellow waymark. Once through onto the gated track, it is no distance to Dale View Farm. There you turn up right through the outer farmyard and left onto an access lane leading to the public road a little north of Westerdale village.

A wide grass verge provides an alternative to tarmac and you quickly reach the River Esk adjacent to Hunter Stee packhorse bridge. Several hump-backed bridges built for packhorses can be found in Esk Dale, among them Duck Bridge near Danby, and Beggars Bridge

Westerdale — perched on the frontier of wild, uninhabitable country.

near Glaisdale. Their distinctive high arches and, in this case, ribbed understructure, gave great strength and rigidity in the days before steel and concrete. In conjunction with paved causeways, they formed vital thoroughfares for the transportation of salted fish and wool to West Riding markets.

As you walk more steeply uphill to Wester-dale village, you pass the youth hostel (though it is set back on the right)—once a romantically sited shooting lodge for Victorian sportsmen who came to bag grouse on the adjacent moors. More than most places in the North York Moors National Park, Westerdale has always struck me as being perched on the very frontier of wild, uninhabitable country—an impression heightened, no doubt, by its diminutive size.

We are now bound for Castleton Rigg whose swelling skyline beckons to the east. To leave Westerdale you turn left along a lane at the top of the village and almost instantly turn right, striking diagonally across two fields linked by stone stiles. You next meet Broad Gate Road, a farm track, and, maintaining a south-easterly direction, follow it down to a small footbridge spanning Tower Beck. Ahead, the boundary wall leads up to Dale Head Farm; staying right of the buildings, a bridleway slants up the steep rim of Castleton Rigg and delivers you to the moor road at High Crag.

Walking apart, there are many fine drives over the North York Moors, the best often traversing long fingers of land which point south and north from the central moorland block. Outside the main holiday season—even within it except at weekends—traffic is relatively light, so these ribbons of tarmac offer satisfactory conditions for walkers, in moderation at least. Some, of course, have been built over ancient trackways, since ridge tops gave firm going for horse-drawn waggons and coaches.

I recommend you cross the road to the rocky outcrop of High Crag, for below and beyond stretches the pastoral scenery of Danby Dale. It is a well sheltered valley supporting small but prosperous farms. Directly opposite you, scattered over wooded hillside, lies the Camphill Trust village of Botton, to be encountered later.

You now stride south along the moortop road for just over half a mile (1.1km) to where the road bends right. Here a post indicates the start of a narrow, indistinct path on the left which rises gently over open moor, effectively continuing your course due south. Passing the occasional boundary stone and Western Howe burial mounds, it arrives at the minor moor road from Rosedale Abbey and the unmistakable, squat shape of Fat Betty.

This old wayside cross at the conjunction of Danby, Westerdale and Rosedale parishes, half limewashed and faintly reminiscent of a rotund

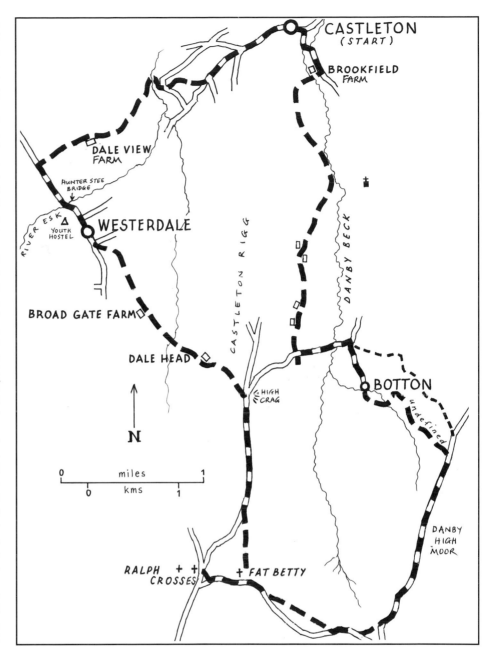

personage, is distinguished from another 'White Cross' near Commondale by its adopted name (it is also known locally as Margery Moorpout). The original wheelhead cross now stands on its weathered base rather than atop a stone shaft. In a landscape bereft of conspicuous features, such structures become a focus of interest for the walker and even an object of affection after several visits.

Acting as navigational aids and sources of spiritual reassurance in times when travelling over the moors would have held far more terrors than today, crosses also marked meeting places for farmers and traders. Not surprisingly, they are often found beside old roadways and

near parish boundaries: even so, their medieval origins remain surrounded by enigma and mystery and some may have replaced standing stones of even greater antiquity.

About 500m to the west, at the summit of a 1409ft (429m) pass, stand Ralph crosses, young and old; if time is in hand, a diversion to look at them is well worth making. Young Ralph Cross, 9ft (2.7m) high and incorporated into the National Park logo, marks the intersection of roads from Westerdale, Castleton, Rosedale Abbey and Gillamoor. The custom of leaving coins in the cup-like depression on top of the cross to help less fortunate wayfarers caused an accidental breakage in 1961: a man climbing to retrieve what coins there might have been toppled the cross which broke into 3 pieces. It was subsequently repaired and reinstated by the then Ministry of Works (now the Department of the Environment).

Two hundred metres or so farther west on slightly higher ground, Old Ralph Cross may mark an older road from Westerdale to Blakey Ridge. In any event, it is an altogether less imposing affair, rougher hewn and of lowlier stature.

Half way back to Fat Betty on the moor road there is a splendid panoramic viewpoint and an accompanying pull-in for motorists. Five hundred metres beyond, where the road swings right, a good track forks off left just before a water-filled hollow. It makes a beeline south-east, short cutting the road which is rejoined for 250m. Another path on the left cuts across the road junction ahead (if in doubt you simply turn left there) and brings you over Seavey Hill onto the gently descending, north-facing slopes of Danby High Moor.

I have never encountered more than an occasional passing vehicle on this high-level B road; walking here can seem peacefully off the beaten track. Hikers on any of several long-distance itineraries use the bridleway on the right which passes Trough House and rounds the head of Great Fryup Dale. Its neighbour, Danby Dale,

Left: **Danby Dale from High Crag.**

Right: **Young Ralph Cross — a much-visited symbol of the North York Moors.**

lies down to your left, while bands of heather and grasses undulate like coloured swells in a static ocean to far horizons. In good visibility, the sharks-fin profile of Roseberry Topping peeps over intervening ridges.

A fraction under a mile (1500m) past the Trough House track, eyes must be peeled for a smallish boulder on the left opposite an overgrown and rutted track on the right (Map Ref: 705 034). You strike off left here on the most tentative of paths over heather, but the way is soon confirmed by a heap of stones and a sunken groove—the original bridleway so confidently marked on maps!

It may be prudent to set a compass bearing of 330 degrees magnetic over the featureless heather to locate a continuation of the bridleway groove, but you will not go far wrong if you stay roughly parallel and above the valley of Old Hannah's Nick. The way soon drops more steeply towards Botton, now in view, passes through a waymarked gate and over pasture above an old wall to a timber footbridge. Following a plantation edge, you go over a stile and left down by a stream, swinging round on a track to Falcon Farm, one of four belonging to Botton village community. Through the farmyard you turn right onto a metalled lane and right over Old Hannah's Nick to the central complex of buildings.

(If you miss all this, do not despair! Just 250m further along the moor road at a pile of stones, another rather unconvincing trod leaves northwest over the heather, heading towards crags on the rim of Danby Rigg, just visible ahead. This path drops into a hollow way, downhill through rampant bracken towards a copse. At a signpost by the intake wall, you turn left through a gate and walk down to Botton Farm; from the lane end, Botton village is reached by turning left.)

As visitors soon discover, Botton is no ordinary village. Since 1955 it has evolved as a working community based around the needs of mentally handicapped adults. A new order of caring has been established, free from 'staff' and 'patient' distinctions. About a third of the inhabitants are not handicapped and it is they who, as fellow workers, co-ordinate activities and help in the successful operation of various enterprises.

Botton village workshops include a bakery producing organic bread and cakes, a creamery renowned for its cheeses, a woodwork shop in which trees become wooden toys, a printing press handling work for outside clients as well as Botton's own publicity material, a weavery producing hand-made rugs and cloths from Botton sheep, and other workshops producing hand-engraved glassware, hand-sewn dolls and hand-made candles. In addition, there are four farms, vegetable gardens and a forestry section.

This tranquil community, set on a picturesque hillside, represents a major step forward in society's attitude to the mentally handicapped.

Before moving on, why not look around? Some units are too far flung for the walker passing through, but you will find a coffee shop, Post Office, gift and book shops in the central complex.

A lane leads north towards Danby and soon meets the dale road. You turn left over Danby Beck and walk uphill past a telephone box and a small Wesleyan Chapel, circa 1855. At Stormy Hall Farm you take to a bridleway on the right by a millstone and turn your back on Danby Head for an increasingly agricultural return leg to Castleton!

The firm, stony track passes through Blackmires Farm and onwards to West Cliff Farm, all the while overshadowed by the lofty edge of Castleton Rigg rising to Brown Hill's long summit (1076ft/328m). Waymarked and provided with wall stiles, the way leads past a rowan tree and into a grassy, walled lane; beyond Plum Tree Farm's yard and along to West Green Farm it is surfaced.

From the T-junction ahead, you could detour right for a visit to Danby's church. An interesting structure containing features from many centuries, it is surprisingly far removed from the present day village, suggesting, perhaps, a much more widely dispersed congregation in earlier times.

You pass through gates above Danby Beck and squelch over boggy ground, further gates leading you uphill away from the stream; Castleton is now visible on its ridge. After crossing a large field you arrive at a signpost and the ensuing bridleway heads up towards Brookfield Farm and into its farmyard. At Wandels Lane, a left turn along the slopes of Danby Low Moor will bring you back to the walk's starting point.

WALK 12: *The Moors Centre, Ainthorpe Rigg and Little Fryup Dale*

Terrain: Rough moorland and daleside paths and some country lanes. Several ups and downs. **Start/Finish:** Danby Lodge Moors Centre.
Distance: 7 miles (11.5km)—allow about 3 hours. **Maps:** OS Landranger Sheet 94; Outdoor Leisure North-East sheet.

This is one of two walks based on the National Park Moors Centre at Danby Lodge, as appropriate a starting and finishing point as you could hope to find! Neither walk is particularly long (with a little creative map work they could even be amalgamated), but each possesses a unique charm which a leisurely pace will do much to enhance. Also, time can be wiled away productively at the Moors Centre itself, as the following notes will confirm.

Housed in a former shooting lodge half a mile east of Danby village and opened in 1976, the Moors Centre offers visitors an impressive array of facilities and information—all free of charge. Open daily between Easter and October, and on winter weekends, the buildings contain an exhibition area dealing with many aspects of life on the North York Moors, a shop selling books, maps and souvenirs, and a cafeteria.

During the busy summer season a daily programme of illustrated talks is augmented by guided walks, Nature and Family Activity trails and Brass Rubbing. Provided bookings are made in advance, school parties and other groups are welcome. The lodge is surrounded by 13 acres of meadow, woodland, formal gardens and picnic areas bordering the River Esk, so there is plenty of room for everyone! Car parking is free, provision is made for the disabled and children can amuse themselves in an adventure playground.

Armed with this knowledge, it is easy to imagine enjoying a day here without moving a muscle: indeed, the Centre is by no means dedicated exclusively to walkers. Newcomers to the National Park who gravitate to Danby Lodge early on in their visit will gain many an insight into wildlife habitats, history, landscape formation, management of the moorland's sheep and grouse populations, farming and forestry—insights which will whet their appetites for exploration, whether on foot or by car.

I have called at the Moors Centre on several occasions and even in high summer have never found it overcrowded. The Information Centre staff are always helpful and an excellent selection of books, maps and leaflets is stocked, including the National Park's own 'Waymark Walks' series.

From the main entrance gate opposite the car park, you walk onto a path (signed to Danby Castle and Fryup Dale) heading south-west alongside the picnic area and wildflower meadow fence. First the River Esk footbridge then the railway line are crossed and at Easton Lane you turn right to Ainthorpe. Across the river, no distance away, lies Danby village,

associated with Canon Atkinson whose memoirs as a local vicar of 53 years' standing are embodied in his book *40 Years in a Moorland Parish*, a classic of its kind.

Taking the Castleton road, you fork left almost immediately and walk up past the Fox and Hounds Inn and Danby Tennis Club. Where the road swings left, you keep straight ahead on a public bridleway between gorse bushes and uphill onto Ainthorpe Rigg.

'Rigg', derived from Old Norse, is the local name for a broad ridge. These moors are overlaid with a patina of standing stones, cairns, barrows and earthworks, the still-visible remnants of burgeoning human settlement which took place during the Bronze Age around 2500 to 3500 years ago and which was responsible for large-scale clearance of woodlands previously covering much of the region, moortops and all. Evident success in occupying and cultivating upland slopes suggests that a warmer, more hospitable climate then prevailed and that the land was more fertile.

The northern end of Danby Rigg in particular bears traces of an ancient field system and many stone-clearance heaps, burial cairns and funerary circles, possibly cremation cemeteries. As you continue up over the moor, one such feature appears close by the path—a standing monolith surrounded by the remains of a large stone circle.

In some contrast, I found myself on tenterhooks during a walk here one August as thousands of honey bees buzzed across the heather collecting nectar. Investigating my bright blue jacket as a prospective flower, they engulfed me in numbers which, as someone not accustomed to bees, I found distinctly unnerving! As a matter of course, you will encounter rows of hives here and there in the Park; some 6000 are installed every summer, each containing upwards of 40,000 bees. In a good year, as many as 120,000 jars of rich, dark honey are produced.

A good track through bracken angles down Crossley Side and delivers you to a road junction near Slate Hill House. Grassy levels and the intake wall attract many sheep who nonchalantly assume precedence over motor traffic! Ahead, the road dips, crosses a cattle grid and Little Fryup Beck and ascends past Stonebeck Gate Farm. About 200m beyond the buildings, you take to a walled, green lane on the left, pass through a gate and turn right up towards a copse of Scots Pine. You keep below it along delightful, brackeny hillside, gaining height to attain the steep edge of Heads overlooking the entire length of Little Fryup Dale.

Once opposite Forester's Lodge below, you fork right on a less distinct track which trends away from the hill's rim through bracken; it passes a marshy spring and gradually veers left

to a wall gate above Crag Wood. You turn right here into a field alongside the wood's upper boundary, following its easterly curve above Danby Crag to Head House. Just before reaching the building, you must aim half-left down to a wooden gate and walk along the bridleway outside the property's north wall.

A left turn is now made downhill over rough ground to join an earthy track turning left to a wall corner. This wall is shadowed through a gate and forward into rampant bracken. During the summer months when undergrowth in general is at its densest—especially in sheltered locations such as this—it seems to be the passage of horses along these tracks and bridleways, rather than walkers, that keeps them open as thoroughfares.

Our onward way enters Crag Wood. It is an ancient, uncleared swath of natural woodland containing a wide variety of broadleaved species, among them oak, birch, hazel and holly. The path is paved—part of an old packhorse way, so many of which criss-cross the North York Moors—and there are several almost magical glades. Contrasts with the sterile monotony of conifer plantations could hardly be drawn more sharply.

All too soon you emerge from the wood to confront a conspicuous signpost. Though not immediately clear on the ground, you keep straight on past a tree and down to a gate where a track to the left of Crag Farm connects with the farm access lane. This will take you across the River Esk to the main valley road (Lawns Road), thankfully not a busy one and therefore pleasant enough for walkers to use.

Instead of following it to the right beneath the railway bridge and directly back to the Moors Centre, I recommend carrying straight on where, in 200m, you reach Duck Bridge. Without doubt it is one of the finest examples of a packhorse bridge to be found in the National Park. Although built centuries ago for teams of pannier-laden horses, it retains sufficient intrinsic strength through its steep-arched design to take the occasional passing car. I have driven over it but with misgivings, for the acute apex threatens to ground a car's chassis!

With an hour or so to spare, you would do well to visit Danby Castle, a quarter-hour's stroll up the lane to the left. Don't expect guided tours, however, as most of the building is now a farm! Put up in the fourteenth century as a palace-fortress by William, Lord Latimer, its layout centres around a courtyard with towers at each corner. With a little imagination, its former splendour, in a commanding position above the dale, can well be appreciated. Two centuries after its founding, Danby Castle and its adjoining lands would be owned by the family of Catherine Parr, sixth wife of Henry VIII and

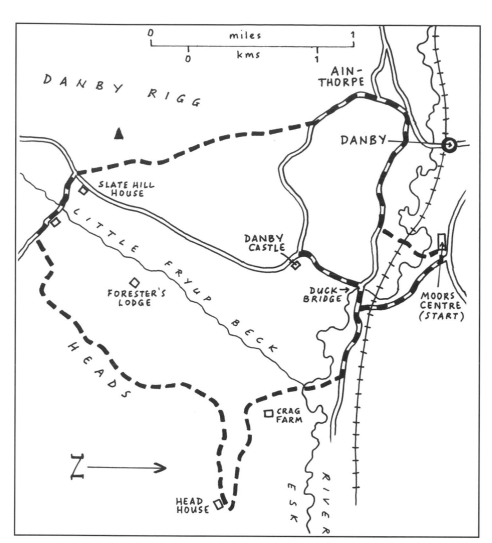

the only one to outlive him.

Danby Estate business such as the settling of grazing rights disputes, is still determined by the manorial Court Leet which convenes in a small room above the main building (a key to view may be obtained from the farmer).

Back at Duck Bridge you have two options for the short return leg to the Moors Centre: either a left turn towards Ainthorpe to rejoin the path over railway and river used when you set out; or, slightly shorter, right then left along the valley road.

Looking back to the long skyline of Ainthorpe Rigg.

54

WALK 13: *Moors Centre, Oakley Walls and Danby Beacon*

Terrain: Country roads, fields, paths and a stony moortop track. **Start/Finish:** Danby Lodge Moors Centre. **Distance:** 7 miles (11.5m)—allow about 3 hours. **Maps:** OS Landranger Sheet 94; Outdoor Leisure North-East sheet.

Second of the walks from Danby Lodge Moors Centre, this itinerary sets out to explore the high land flanking Esk Dale to the north and culminating in Danby Beacon. There are classic views over the broad valley bottom to the two Fryup dales bounded by the bleak, distant horizons of Glaisdale and Danby moors.

For details of the Moors Centre, please see Walk 12. From the car park you walk south-east down the road and in about 250m turn left over a stile at a footpath sign. Diagonally across the field, in its top right-hand corner, a gate provides access along to Park House. The name 'Park' crops up frequently in this part of the Esk valley, reminding us that wooded deer parks occupied substantial tracts of the valley sides from the fourteenth century (when Danby Castle was built), supplying game for the hunting gentry. It is possible that Danby Lodge was this park's main entrance, for it extended east from Crow Wood to Houlsyke village and accounts for all those straight-line enclosure walls on Oakley Side between arable land bordering the Esk and exposed moorland higher up.

Continuing ahead through a farmyard, you meet the back road at a hairpin bend and keep ahead past Oakley Side House. Where the road begins to dip towards Houlsyke, you turn left, cross a ladder stile and walk uphill to the right of a wall on a Concessionary Path. At the unfenced moor road near Oakley Walls Farm 260ft (80m) higher, you turn right and are soon gently descending above a maze of field enclosures bordering Esk Dale. I have yet to find the many pathways shown as hatched lines on the 1:25,000 map weaving up over the moor towards Danby Beacon. A fringe of bracken must be climbed across before you gain any impression of what lies above and even then the hillside shows few signs of ever being walked. If you wanted a short-cut and can navigate accurately by compass, rights-of-way on the map could be followed, but the going is awkward through dense heather.

More agreeable by far is a continuing stroll above Oakley Walls, from which vantage point a geology lesson comes to life! Twelve thousand years ago, towards the end of the last Ice Age, glacial ice blocked the meltwater channels at Kirkdale and Lealholm, flooding Esk Dale and adjacent Fryup and Danby dales to about the 700ft (213m) contour. Sediments laid down on the bed of this huge glacial lake produced rich soils after the ice had retreated, witness the crops and meadowland below.

Soon after passing Park Wood and Greystone farms, the road swings right and starts to drop in earnest towards Lealholm. Walkers wishing to visit this attractive village (perhaps returning to Danby by train as an alternative to the high level return leg of this route) can happily do so,

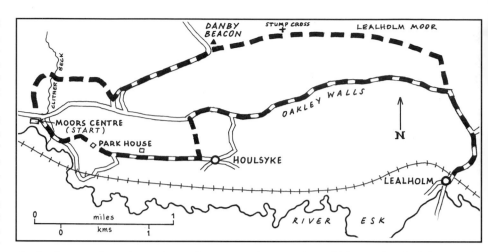

for the descent takes only 15 minutes. However, should you then intend to resume the walk, a climb back up of some 300ft (90m) from the valley bottom is entailed.

If you have the time and the necessary puff, don't miss Lealholm! It is one of those comparatively rare places that exudes picturesque charm yet manages to resist making too many overtures to the visiting tourist. Having said that, there are picnic areas, a tea room, an inn, a few shops, a village green and a car park, but it is the Esk—here a wide, babbling river overhung with trees and home to ducks—that holds centre stage. On the wall of the Wesleyan Chapel near the river stepping stones are recorded the flood levels of 1840 and 1930, when the Esk showed its other, destructive, face.

Continuing from the road bend on Lealholm Moor, you turn north up a good stony track at the bend sign and in 500m turn left; this is a T-junction near Stick-i'-th'-Mire Bog, though memories of actual danger to travellers here are lost in the mists of time! With underfoot conditions in fact clear and firm, fast progress is possible and views south to upper Glaisdale and Great Fryup Dale are far-ranging.

Little by little you gain height as you approach Brown Rigg End and you should be watching out for Stump Cross on your right. In common with the majority of moorland crosses, its shaft-top and crosspiece are missing, yet its obvious antiquity arouses one's curiosity. Those who have encountered 'Fat Betty' on the moors south of Castleton may notice a striking resemblance (see Walk 11). This is the old road from Whitby to the west and Stump Cross almost certainly marks the intersection with a road branching north to Scaling.

Eyes will now be fixed firmly on the tall marker post atop Danby Beacon's tumulus, at just under 1000ft (299m) above sea level and only half a mile away. Adjacent ground sprawls vaguely downhill but there is no real sense of elevation and in poor visibility it is a disappoint-

ing summit at which to arrive. Only in clear air does a 360 degree panorama unfold, from Kildale in the west to Goathland in the east, south to the high moors above the Fryup dales and north over Scaling Reservoir and the busy Whitby to Guisborough road to distant Teesside.

Leaving the beacon, you walk the moor road in a south-west direction for just over 1km, ignoring a left fork. In a further 200m you strike off sharp right onto a footpath and follow it downhill to the right of a wall.

On your right now, the hillside is peppered with coal workings from the eighteenth and nineteenth centuries. Around 40 miners were employed in the pits, producing coal for the burning of lime quarried at nearby Commondale and spread liberally throughout the dale to sweeten the acid soils.

The wall swings left above Rudsdales Nursery and leads to Clither Beck. Once over the stream you bear half-left uphill and pass through a field gate into a small wood. All that remains is to walk south to meet the road at the back of the Moors Centre buildings.

Below: **Stump Cross.**

Above: **The River Esk at Lealholm.**

Right: **Looking south from above Oakley Walls.**

Far right: **Danby Beacon.**

The hardy Swaledale — grazer of the high moors.

WALK 14: *A Circuit of Glaisdale*

Terrain: Moor and daleside tracks and paths, including two moderate ups and downs. Map reading useful in places. **Start/Finish:** Upper Glaisdale village. **Distance:** 9½ miles (15km)—allow 4 to 5 hours. **Maps:** OS Landranger Sheet 94; Outdoor Leisure North-East sheet.

Glaisdale belongs to a row of valleys which thrust, finger-like, from Esk Dale south into the central moorland massif. Originally an ironstone miners' village, Glaisdale has added a crop of modern housing to its old grey terraces stacked against steep hillsides overlooking the River Esk. Most visitors gravitate to Beggars Bridge and East Arncliff Wood near the railway station at the village's lower end. Walkers, however, have a marvellous outing in prospect by following this route which explores the contrasting north and south dalesides and dips across Glaisdale Head.

From the village top (The Green) you set off south-west past houses and through gates, out onto the lower slopes of Glaisdale Rigg. 'Rigg' appears widely as a topographical feature on maps and is an old Norse word for 'broad ridge'. Keeping along the main track past overgrown quarry workings, you reach a water-filled hollow at the conjunction of several pathways and here fork right on a clear green track ascending the moorside at a gentle gradient. This is the old Whitby Road, unsuitable for motor vehicles but providing a splendid 1½ miles (2.5km) of firm going for pedestrians.

As Glaisdale Low Moor, a broad saddle of rough, tawny pasture gradually gives way to the more pronounced shoulder of Glaisdale Rigg, you will pass several inscribed stones by the wayside—milestones and boundary markers from days when the old road was busy with horse-drawn coaches and waggons. Views across the dale reveal large plantations of mixed woodland, a feature absent from other south-pointing valleys west of Newton Dale.

An OS pillar at 1070ft (326m) above sea level pinpoints the summit of Glaisdale Rigg and stands about 50m away beside the modern road from Lealholm. This ribbon of tarmac swings right round Glaisdale Head and although it could be walked as a longer alternative to the ensuing down-and-up traverse, it cannot be recommended. Few walkers enjoy the unrelieved hardness and there is a big 'dog-leg' corner adding distance to be covered before reaching Wintergill Plantation—unless, that is, you fancy navigating by compass over boggy Traverse Moor!

Not that the initial section of what follows is wholly straightforward! At my last visit the path was narrow and prone to obscurity beneath bracken in high summer. A little way back from the Lealholm road at an 'Unsuitable for Motors' sign, you take to an overgrown bridleway heading off south. A pipe connected by concrete inspection chambers is crossed and a ruined barn (Red House) aimed for at a stand of trees. Here you turn left downhill beside a wall, through more bracken and field gates and forward to trees.

Once on the dale road over Hardhill Beck

and past Yew Grange, this charming valley lane bordered with foxgloves leads you past Hob Garth, an exquisite stone house and colourful garden. The intimacy of field and settlement, of gill and copse, in this sheltered dalehead acts as a foil for sterner reaches of path up on the moorland rim: ample recompense for the legwork involved!

Swinging left and climbing, the lane approaches the renovated cottages of Mountain Ash Farm. Just above it you pass through the middle of three gates and walk up a walled green track. The going gets steeper through the field ahead, at whose top you bear right below a television aerial (reception must cause a few headaches in this part of the world!). Now in a hollow groove, you are following a big zig-zag near Wintergill Plantation towards open hillside, but at the plantation wall there is an interruption in the otherwise clear path. To overcome it you strike left over grassy terrain between banks of bracken to where the way becomes re-established over heather on Nab Rigg.

With the intake wall visible ahead, the moor-top is attained in a few minutes. Wild, lonely horizons sweep the eye from south-east to south-west. Roads—even paths—are few and far between and apart from hikers on the Lyke Wake Walk and one or two other challenging routes, these infinities of heather in the National Park's heartland are rarely trodden by humans. Indeed, wandering off existing rights-of-way is to be discouraged in principle, for much of the Park is in private ownership and access has had to be negotiated.

The pleasant track dips to Winter Gill near a derelict sheepfold—a pretty enough place at which to break the walk before commencing the return leg. In 200m you arrive at the high road linking Rosedale with Esk Dale and turn left alongside it to the far end of Wintergill Plantation. Here an obvious track shadows the plantation edge to a corner where it is necessary to strike off half-right on a thinner trod passing between a cairn and an upright marker stone. Many such stones can be found around Glaisdale Head, some bearing curious inscriptions from the early eighteenth century.

Only as progress is made towards the convex moor edge do views of Glaisdale truly open out, but even before then distant skylines impart a vivid sense of space. More walkers get lost in farmland than on the tops and the next stretch invites careful route-finding if that particular ignominy is to be avoided! As is usually the case, it is intricacies in field layout—the positioning of walls, tracks and gates—that cause confusion, rather than footpath lines on a map, which often appear deceptively straightforward.

As the path drops, you fork right through dense heather, down by a groove to a wall and fence where a gate leads to brackeny slopes above Low Gill Beck Farm. Descending left of the buildings by a duck pond, you reach the dale road. Guidebook instructions read poorly in what purports to be an appreciation of a walk.

Ruined sheepfold at Winter Gill.

Suffice to say that you pass New House and Bank House farms before taking to field paths and crossing two streams. Glaisdale Beck is spanned by a good footbridge and the climb towards Red house on the outskirts of Glaisdale village is distinguished by sections of paved causeway running between hedges.

Stone causeways are encountered frequently in the National Park, though many have disappeared beneath new roads or have been destroyed by culverting and recent trackways. For centuries they were the arteries and capillaries along which commodities of all kinds moved to keep, as it were, the collective body of dispersed communities alive and thriving. Teams of up to 40 pack ponies laden with wicker panniers could carry more weight over rougher terrain than any wheeled waggon and until the advent of railway transport and turnpike roads they provided the chief means of communication. Causeway slabs are invariably worn hollow by the passage of countless hooves over several centuries of use: interestingly, similar paving often represents the best way to prevent serious erosion on today's footpaths where high densities of visitors are expected.

There are consistently fine retrospective views over the dale as you enter the lane below Red House. The walk is all but over and within 500m you have passed St Thomas' Church and regained the centre of Glaisdale Village.

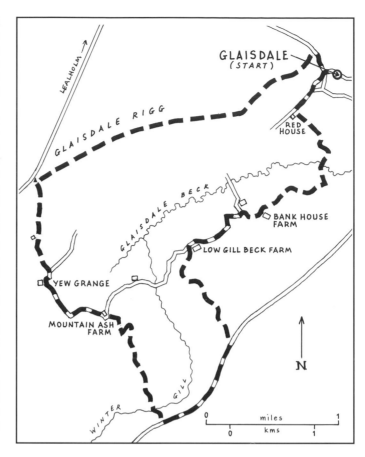

Facing page: **Whitby harbour from above the Old Town on the south bank of the River Esk.**

Left: **Looking across to Glaisdale Head from the descent to Low Gill Beck Farm.**

Below: **The slopes of Glaisdale Rigg from the dale head.**

WALK 15: *The Coast from Staithes to Whitby*

Terrain: A clear, undulating path along rugged, eroding cliffs with one or two moderate ascents. Some beach walking and a little road work at high tides. **Start:** Staithes—accommodation or return transport arrangements will be necessary as this is a linear walk. **Finish:** Whitby. **Distance:** 12 miles (19km)—allow about 6 hours (longer if delayed by high water at Runswick Bay). **Maps:** OS Landranger Sheet 94; Outdoor Leisure North-East sheet.

After many visits, I have formed the conclusion that what the Yorkshire coast may lack by comparison with the warmer, more salubrious south and west of Britain is amply compensated for by a different, sterner kind of beauty.

In many places, scars of the alum, ironstone and jet industries disfigure the landscape, yet rapid marine erosion gnawing away at the coast detracts from any picturesque attractiveness anyway. These great, slipping faces of soft shales and boulder clay falling to a rocky foreshore, frequently assailed by bitter easterly gales and pounded by a bullying North Sea, possess a certain dour grandeur.

Perversely, the walk may not reveal its true character on balmy days of warm sunshine and blue skies. Stormy, changeable weather with animated light and rough seas will enhance your appreciation of this gloriously comfortless stretch of coastline. I vividly recall walking this way one April amid violent squalls. 'Walking' is a misnomer, for it was all but impossible to stay upright at times, though thankfully the gale was behind me. Curtains of snow swept inland across spuming surf and the entire landscape was engulfed in Turneresque streamers of vapour. No fine day, however enjoyable the walking, can compete with such elemental drama or leave so indelible a memory.

Staithes' intimate huddle of tall cottages, stacked in the gorge of Roxby Beck with no room for gardens, is best seen from Cowbar Lane, just before it plunges narrowly towards the harbour. But even from closer perspectives, the old fishing village, half-heartedly protected from the attentions of North Sea waves by Cowbar Nab, deserves a frame or two of your film. In high season, its winding, cobbled streets become clogged with visitors, though vehicular traffic is restricted and you are advised to use the upper car park.

Three hundred local men and women once worked in the fishing industry here; after 1885 their catches were crated out by train to city markets. Eventually, steam trawlers from larger ports monopolised trade and the 120 'cobles' based at Staithes dwindled to the handful we see today. ('Cobles' are open boats unique to the east coast, built on Viking lines with high, sharp bows and wide amidships to deal with heavy surf.) Although substantially given over to tourism, Staithes continues as a crab and lobster fishing port, thus retaining its centuries-long seafaring tradition.

Income was not always legitimately earned and Staithes became something of a centre for smuggling on the Yorkshire coast during the eighteenth and early nineteenth centuries. Contraband, including chocolate, tea, pepper, snuff and playing cards as well as the more familiar spirits, was brought ashore, distributed inland

and sold to the public by highly organised teams of people. Despite the attempts of armed Customs patrols and sometimes violent clashes, black market trade flourished until the government's conversion to the principles of free trade brought about dramatic reductions in duties around the mid-1850s.

Round above the little sandy beach by the Cod and Lobster Inn, its walls reinforced with steel after repeated demolition by the sea—the last time in January 1953—you gain a very real sense of the village's vulnerability, especially if a big sea is running. Houses were often washed away by storm waves until the two breakwaters were constructed; at the time of writing, plans are afoot, I believe, to extend the height of the north one and increase its effectiveness.

On quiet off-season days, it is easy to imagine little has changed here since Captain Cook's days. As a lad in 1744, James Cook served his haberdashery apprenticeship in William Sanderson's shop, since rebuilt in Church Street. Eighteen months later, the sea well and truly in his blood, he began his illustrious career as a Royal Navy navigator and explorer of new lands.

And so to the walk itself! Immediately beyond the Cod and Lobster you turn right up a cul-de-sac, past Captain Cook's cottage, climb steps and turn left up a gully onto the cliff path (way-marked 'Cleveland Way', of which this walk forms a small part). Having thus gained clifftop level near modern farm buildings, the way ahead is clear to see, crossing stiles through fields some distance back from the cliff edge and rising steeply over pasture to a stile and signpost on Beacon Hill (378ft/115m).

Still at over 325ft (99m) above the sea, the ensuing section offers definitive views at low tide down to the vast Lias Limestone 'scars' of Brackenberry Wyke. Such scars are found in many locations and are a distinctive feature of this coast. In no time at all, the path leads to houses and the road end at Port Mulgrave.

Far below, the little harbour is hopelessly choked with stones and mud, its jetty half derelict. Yet, until the ironstone mine at nearby Dalehouse closed in 1916, ore had been transported by rope-hauled wagons from the workings through a mile-long tunnel (now sealed) and shipped from Port Mulgrave to the furnaces of Jarrow.

Where the road to Hinderwell bends right at a sign for the Ship Inn, you turn left and resume clifftop progress along the perimeter of arable fields. Rosedale Wyke, issuing as a waterfall in rainy weather, requires careful footwork to negotiate a slippery little down-and-up. Old fencing below the path at Lingrow Cliffs provides a graphic reminder, if one is needed, of this coast's alarming instability. Indeed, almost the entire original village of Runswick slipped

into the sea one fateful night in 1664.

Being watchful to turn right, inland, at a stile, you will soon reach the Runswick Bay Hotel. From the road junction, you turn left along Bank Top Lane and take the old road, now a track, downhill to a stepped path and thence into Runswick Bay village. By no means uniquely, the community's fortunes hung on fishing in its early days and the industry's decline here mirrors that of nearby Staithes. Smuggling was rife, too, with salvage from shipwrecks, the Kettleness alum quarries and Grinkle ironstone mines bringing, in their own ways, a little consolation in what must often have been abrasively hard times.

Real change at Runswick Bay was wrought by the arrival of the railway and the resulting inexorable shift towards catering for visitors. New houses were built above the bay, locals drifted away, shops closed through lack of regu-

lar custom and by the 1950s the holiday settlement we see today was established. Even so, many original buildings remain—renovated and prettified perhaps, but well worth taking time to admire.

At high tide, the onward route is somewhat problematic and walkers have no realistic alternative but to wait for the beach top to clear. Once I set out, fiercely determined to find a way through the dense scrub and thorn bushes. Before long I found myself among derelict holiday chalets, their walls akimbo, gardens choked with brambles, a lawn mower abandoned, kitchen implements strewn around. Twenty years ago, perhaps, these terrestial *Marie Celestes* were fondly tended, supplied with water and connected by neat pathways, but subsidence eventually won the day.

In the face of huge waves breaking along the

Low-tide 'scars' of Lias Limestone at Brackenberry Wyke.

shoreline bank, I scrambled onto an overgrown track up into fields and emerged, dishevelled, on the cinder trackbed of the old Yorkshire coast railway. None of this rather futile escapade was on public rights of way and I would categorically discourage any similar foray into the landslipped wilderness behind Runswick Sands!

There are steps to the beach near rows of brightly coloured cobles hauled up by tractor onto hard standing by the car park. Once there, you walk east past the Sailing Club to the foot of cliffs ahead where, though silted up, Hob Holes can be made out. Runswick's 'hob' ('hobs', or goblins, feature in many legends of the York-

Above: **Traditional 'cobles' moored in Roxby Beck, Staithes.**

Right: **Old alum quarries on Kettle Ness headland, seen across Runswick Bay.**

Far right: **Walking the beach at Sandsend towards distant Whitby.**

shire moors and dales) was reputed to cure whooping cough!

A hundred metres or so beyond, you climb a stream valley, cross its footbridge and attack the stiff 330ft (100m) stepped ascent of High Cliff. Easier terrain follows and you soon reach Kettleness, a cluster of redbrick houses built for employees of the disused coastal railway. Some 800m to the south-east, reached by road and field path, rises the grassy mound of Scratch Alley Roman Signal Station.

As you might expect for a strategic position, views are wide-ranging. During its operational life in the fourth century, a timber or stone lookout tower stood atop the existing foundations. Good advance warning would have been gained by the Roman forces of any threatened invasion from the North Sea, a vigilance supplemented by other Signal Stations from Hunt Cliff near Saltburn in the north, to Filey Brigg south of Scarborough.

Until it disappears into a boarded-up tunnel, the railway trackbed is closely shadowed by the coast path. You are rising and dipping above high, slumped and eroded cliffs; Keldhowe Point promontory was seriously undermined by jet workings in the nineteenth century when Whitby jet artefacts were in great demand, and has suffered extensive collapse. Once past the

railway tunnel portal, the trackbed leads you through the remains of large alum quarries at Deep Grove and Ness End.

Wildlife has recolonised the quarry workings, waste tips and railway cutting. Birds seen here will include woodcock, snipe, sparrowhawk and green woodpecker, while adjacent marshy areas and woodland support many diverse plant and insect species. For more detailed information about wildlife and about the old alum industry itself, see the North York Moors National Park booklet, *Sandsend Trail.*

The stark, ochre headland of Sandsend Ness, hewn into and reshaped by three centuries of man's labouring, reveals more than a naturally eroded headland would of its geological structure. A complex series of shales overlay jet rock and are capped by boulder clay deposits from the last Ice Age. Seen in retrospect from Sandsend, the Ness's profile, brutalised though it is, has already been softened by the elements and glows appealingly in the sunshine.

I have always had the good fortune to arrive at Sandsend on a low or falling tide, thus avoiding a tiresome 1½ mile (2.5km) trudge alongside the A174 (though the high-water route does thereafter thread interestingly above the shore). Walking the beach does have its own special reward—an hour held between the roaring surf

on one side and countless signs of the sea's awesome power in the form of landslips and smashed sea defences on the other.

There is no finer way to enter Whitby, the epitome of east coast fishing ports, than to have walked there beside the sea which is both its *raison d'être* and its age-old adversary. No Yorkshire community is more vigorous nor more steeped in seafaring associations: even the amusement arcades, the ice cream and candy floss, the fish and chips and razzmatazz which it heartily dispenses to summer trippers fail to eclipse the serious business of putting to sea. In really rough weather, the twin harbour entrance piers and the narrow, awkward channel they protect become a compulsive focus of attention.

I never tire of visiting Whitby, though, Folk Festival apart, I confess to preferring it out of season. Describing its many attractions lies outside the scope of this book, but make a point if you can of seeing the fish quay, the Lifeboat Station, the old town on the River Esk's east bank beneath the Abbey ruins, Captain Cook's life and times in the Pannet Park Museum and the little gallery of century-old local photographs by Frank Meadow Sutcliffe which provide fascinating glimpses into Whitby's past.

Whitby lifeboat.

WALK 16: *From Glaisdale to Robin Hood's Bay*

Terrain: Every kind, from valley lanes and tracks to woodland, riverside, moorland and cliff paths. Some road walking and a few considerable gradients. Map and compass necessary in places. **Start:** Beggars Bridge, Glaisdale. **Finish:** The North Sea, Robin Hood's Bay. **Distance:** 19 miles (31km)—allow a full day, approximately 10 hours. Shorter alternatives suggested. **Maps:** OS Landranger Sheet 94; Outdoor Leisure North-East sheet.

Unlike the majority of classic walks in the main section of this book, Glaisdale to the coast is a linear route. There is no denying it makes a long day out and is likely, therefore, to be attempted by the more experienced and fitter souls among us. However, I would certainly not discourage anyone from setting off, for not only do untold delights await you, but it is feasible to cut short the walk at several points if so desired. It is, without doubt, a very fine hike in terms of variety, incorporating virtually all the landscape features for which the National Park is renowned: moor, woodland, river valley and coast.

It will become apparent that, as on Alfred Wainwright's Coast to Coast Walk which treads similar ground on its final leg to the North Sea from St Bees in Cumbria, I have chosen to approach Robin Hood's Bay along the cliff path. In fact, 5 miles (8km) could be saved by taking to the road but, I suggest, only as a last resort, for the detour round to the coast path forms a magnificent climax to the walk.

Glaisdale's sturdy, slate-roofed terraced houses bordering its steep village street were built for ironstone miners and their families after ore deposits were discovered around 1868 on moors to the south-west—in truth only a few miles from the industry's hub in Rosedale. Three blast-furnaces were operational here in Glaisdale, continuing a history of smelting which dates back to 1223, but fierce competition from cheaper imports closed the ironworks in 1876 after a life of only 8 years.

For the visiting walker it is a confusing place, half centred around the few shops on the hill, half around the railway station down at Carr End by the River Esk. The latter is to be our starting point, more specifically Beggars Bridge (Map Ref: 784 055).

During the Middle Ages, long before the advent of such materials as steel and concrete, bridges to take packhorse trains across rivers were built using a high stone arch incorporating an acute-angled central key stone. The method proved incredibly robust, witness the fine condition of Beggars Bridge which had already been rebuilt in 1620! Somewhat overshadowed by the adjacent railway bridge, it is nevertheless an immensely pleasing and elegant structure, especially in evening light when its mellow stone glows warmly against a backcloth of trees bordering the Esk. There is a pull-in by the road as well as a nearby car park and countless tourists stop here to stroll and take the obligatory snapshot!

Top: **Sunset from Sleights Moor.**

Facing page: **Beggars Bridge.**

Bottom: **Walkers descending from Flat Howe towards the Littlebeck valley.**

The walk starts by passing beneath the railway bridge and crossing Glaisdale Beck by footbridge. You have swung left and initially there is a steep climb as the path enters East Arncliff Wood, but before long you descend temporarily to the riverside. Gaining height once more, you will notice underfoot a paved causeway of sandstone slabs, originally laid for packhorse trains—the juggernauts of three centuries ago! There are many such causeways in the North York Moors (some are featured in classic walks), and there can be little doubt that communications and trade between communities relied upon them: hooves and feet could pass in all weathers regardless of surrounding terrain. When, in recent years, slabs were lifted for turning, it was discovered that their undersides were also worn, indicating a previous turning by our ancestors to improve the way many years ago!

East Arncliff Woods are particularly beautiful in springtime and autumn, but even in winter, when vegetation is dormant and branches bare, there are compensations: obscured by foliage at other times, views then open out over precipitous hillsides to the fast-flowing Esk and the valley railway.

Broadleaved trees on all sides show signs of having been 'coppiced'—that is, felled to encourage the growth on new shoots from the

Falling Foss in springtime.

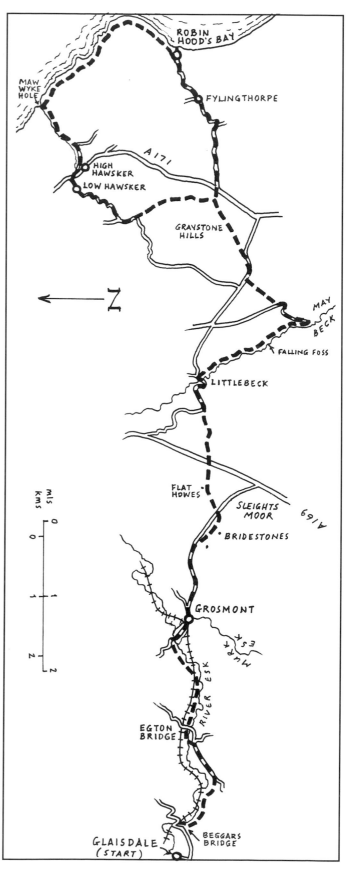

stump. Such young timber once provided an invaluable source of fencing poles, charcoal and firewood. Alder and sycamore were used to fashion clogs, the predominant footwear in the mills of Yorkshire and Lancashire, and a thriving local industry existed here before World War I.

After more undulations, the path emerges onto a by-road at Delves (actually the moor road from Rosedale). You turn down left and follow it towards Egton Bridge where, just past the Horseshoe Inn, stepping stones cross the River Esk. In times of spate you may be forced to continue ahead to the road bridge. Two hundred metres along to the left stands a Roman Catholic Church, unexceptional architecturally but distinguished by a row of coloured bas-relief panels on its exterior walls. In common with most of mid-Eskdale, scenery around Egton Bridge is a delight, including a wealth of majestic trees such as the Sequoias in the Egton Estate grounds.

Our onward route now turns east, almost opposite the Catholic Church, onto the old toll road—a private estate road open to pedestrians—which passes Beckside Farm and the original toll bar where a sign displays the tolls formerly charged (Hearses 6d!). Flanking the river, you soon reach the Egton-Grosmont road, turning right over the bridge and bidding farewell to the Esk as you cross.

Grosmont is the North York Moors Historical Railway's northern terminus and something of a mecca for steam train enthusiasts. It is also the starting point for an Historical Railway Trail covered by Walk 17 and is thus described in more detail there. Should you already be considering a return to Glaisdale, now is your best chance for an early retreat: just north of the village centre stands a British Rail station on the scenic Esk Valley line, though—be warned—trains are not that frequent! I hope you arrive at Grosmont when there is steam train activity—it is blood-stirring stuff!

Loins will need girding up for the 1 in 3 ascent onto Sleights Moor. Left forks are ignored as you climb Fair Head Lane for the better part of a mile before attaining open moor at a cattle grid. A detour to the right leads to Low Bride Stones, all but lost in a marshy hollow, then, keeping parallel to the road, to High Bride Stones which are somewhat more intact. Views west from this moorland brow are impressive, embracing all the country so far walked and horizons beyond.

In poor visibility you will need a compass, as the way now lies over trackless heather (a touch north of east), crosses the road and aims for the ancient burial mound of Flat Howe. In a topographical sense it is the walk's turning point, though not yet half way, for the coast is in sight, Whitby and its Abbey silhouetted against the

sea, Robin Hood's Bay a cliffline dip to the right.

Southwards, the incongruous three 'golf balls' of Fylingdales Ballistic Missile Early Warning Station strike a discordant note amidst such beauty and tranquillity, reminding us perhaps of man's darker preoccupations with political power and of the slender thread upon which civilised life sometimes seems to hang.

On the same easterly course, you strike off over gently dipping heather: if nothing else, it will polish your boots up incomparably well! The busy A169 Whitby to Pickering road, already within sight and earshot, is crossed and a rough track taken opposite, signposted to Littlebeck. At first over muddy, stony slopes, it enters a lane and is joined by the road from Sleights for a steep descent to Littlebeck hamlet—one of those lanes you are glad to be walking down, not driving!

Littlebeck appears idyllically lovely at many times of the year, but never more so than in spring when flowers embroider banks and gardens with traceries of colour. Its Arcadian delights, however, do not date back further than the last century when local alum quarries finally ceased operation. Alum was extracted from shale through a complex process of heating and distillation and was used extensively in the paper making, hide tanning and textile dyeing industries. Littlebeck, a centre for alum quarrying along with Sandsend and Ravenscar on the coast, still bears the overgrown scars of its industrial past in pathside spoil heaps and exposed shaley slopes among the trees.

The path now follows Little Beck upstream towards Falling Foss from just below a house at the road bend. There are twists and turns and branches off to the left, but the main woodland track uphill is clear enough, passing old quarries and reaching a massive boulder. Hewn out as a shelter by a mason named Jeffrey, it is beautifully inscribed 'The Hermitage' and 'G.C. 1790', believed to refer to George Chubb, a Littlebeck schoolmaster involved in the construction of nearby Newton House.

A little farther on you skirt the stone wall perimeter of Newton House, once a shooting lodge but now an Outdoor Pursuits Centre, and drop to Falling Foss. As waterfalls go it is not a high one, but few can compare with its delectable setting in an intimate bowl of deciduous forest. Across the footbridge in front of Midge Hall (the aptly named Keeper's Cottage!), you walk about 60m upstream to a stone bridge but stay on the right bank where you are soon able to cross May Beck on stepping stones to gain a clear path on the other side. (After heavy rain when the beck may be in spate, you will need to return to the stone bridge and walk up the track to find a higher level path on the right joining up with the route ahead).

During the past decade, the Forestry Commission has waymarked Forest Trails within the valley, complete with access roads and car parks at Falling Foss and May Beck. If you happen to arrive using only an old OS map, be prepared for surprises! Closely shadowing May Beck along its sylvan course, you eventually arrive at May Beck picnic area, hugely popular with families on sunny summer days.

Doubling back north from the bridge, a tarmac road leads you up past New May Beck Farm. Beyond the left-hand bend you veer off north-east across Sneaton Low Moor to the B1416 at the end of a plantation belt. More straightforward but duller to walk, a gated road opposite (Raikes' Lane) winds and undulates through a landscape of upland fields to Hawsker, our next objective. Recommended if time and energy allow is the continuation described below which, in fact, holds the key to a short-cut by road direct to Robin Hood's Bay should circumstances dictate an early finale.

Turning right alongside the often busy B1416 for about 600m (thank goodness for wide verges!), you fork off left at a gate onto the indeterminate heathery plateau of Graystone Hills. You may, as I have done, confirm the map-marked bridleway by compass, but I doubt you will find a corresponding trod! Grooves and hollows suggest traces of a former path, though you are best navigating through young or burned heather where the going is easiest. With luck you will pass the remains of a stone cross and approach the main Scarborough to Whitby road (A171).

Robin Hood's Bay lies just 2 miles (3.2km) east via Fylingthorpe on the facing B road. It's downhill all the way and there are fine coastal views, but any route which road traffic, too, can take is bound to lack those special perspectives unique to walking ways. In this case you would also miss a good section of cliff path and the insight it provides into coastal erosion—a subject of vital concern to inhabitants of the Yorkshire seaboard.

And so, eschewing a beeline for the sea, we head north, crossing the source of Stony Gate Slack and trending left of a low tumulus. With heather moorland now firmly behind you, a succession of two gates, still on rough terrain, leads to a muddy lane and thence to a corner of country road. A mile away to the right and straddling the A171, Low and High Hawsker stand at the sea's threshold and it is resolutely seaward that the way proceeds, over the main road, along towards Robin Hood's Bay and left on a caravan site lane.

The dismantled Yorkshire Coast Railway—now a Permitted Path for public recreational use—also heads our way, but a couple of bends later you walk down by Oakham Beck through Northcliffe Caravan Park and out to the coast

path above Maw Wyke Hole.

Being part of the long-distance Cleveland Way, the coast path is thoroughly well walked and, as you turn right along it, only stiles and mild gradients interrupt a pleasant sequence of arable field edges above high, rugged cliffs. First the distant bulk of Ravenscar's headland (South Cheek), then the red-roofed huddle of Robin Hood's Bay village hove into sight as you round North Cheek (or Ness Point).

Past the Coastguard Station, striking low-tide 'scars' of rock can be seen extending from the base of soft, boulder-clay cliffs—cliffs that have threatened communities with subsidence and collapse ever since man first settled on the sea's edge. At Robin Hood's Bay alone, some 200 dwellings have been washed away during the past two centuries; even the new sea wall constructed in 1975 is subject to repeated onslaughts by storms and will need constant maintenance.

Through kissing gates the coast path emerges into Mount Pleasant, an estate of houses originally built near the railway station for wealthy seamen and landowners in the village's heyday as a port. Left down Station Road will be found the car park (only local traffic is allowed into

Above: **The red-roofed huddle of Robin Hood's Bay from the coast path just above the village.**

Right: **The last few steps towards the sea are through narrow, picturesque streets.**

Facing page: **Grosmont station — a Pickering train waiting to depart.**

the tortuous, narrow streets) and pedestrian steps leading to the bottom of the hill where the tarmac ends at a rough slipway. There is no shortage of places at which to eat, drink and be merry, nor for that matter at which to spend the night, though in high season it all gets very, very busy.

WALK 17: *The Grosmont Historical Railway Trail*

Terrain: Gentle inclines on the old trackbed; rougher field and woodland paths to return. **Start/Finish:** Grosmont station car park. **Distance:** 6½ miles (10.5km)—allow 3 to 4 hours. **Maps:** OS Landranger Sheet 94; Outdoor Leisure North-East sheet.

Every walk has its story: this one is longer and more fascinating than most. It revolves around one of the North York Moors' great attractions—the privately run steam railway between Grosmont and Pickering. During the summer season when services are at their most frequent, you are never far from the pulsing hiss of steam and it is difficult to imagine a walk of greater appeal to railway enthusiasts. Even those too young for nostalgic associations are moved by the romance and elemental excitement of it all.

Countless holidaymakers undertake the scenic journey from Grosmont, the line's northern terminus, to Pickering or to one of the intermediate stations which act as springboards for walks in the adjacent moors and forests. Yet once installed inside a railway carriage you are largely insulated from the hauling engine; only by embarking upon a walk such as that described below do you gain varied perspectives of the trains as they pass above, beside and beneath you, by woodland and riverside, from distant echo to full-blooded close up.

It all begins at Grosmont, where an entertaining day can be spent watching the trains come and go from a number of excellent viewpoints within half a mile of the village. There is a museum to look at, as well as engine sheds and rolling stock in various stages of repair. Sights and sounds impinge on the senses and even walkers chafing at the bit for some exercise will be tempted to linger!

Except on special Christmas weekends, no trains run between November and March and during the low seasons each side of the June/July/August peak, services diminish to 3 or 4 per day. Whilst reducing or even eliminating your chances of seeing trains, depending on when you set out, compensations include no crowds, stunning views of the moors and woods in spring or autumn garb, and plenty of time to contemplate the history of this extraordinary line.

Grosmont, thronged with steam enthusiasts and holidaymakers on summer weekends, presents us with a very different face to that of 150 years ago when it was an ironstone centre of some importance. Iron had probably been worked in the area as long as 2000 years ago—certainly in medieval times. Interestingly, the industry was to undergo something of a re-birth during the 1830s, but only as a consequence of George Stephenson's railway from Whitby to Pickering. Navvies tunnelling through Lease Rigg unearthed rich seams of iron-bearing ore and companies were rapidly set up to exploit them.

In the spring of 1839, the richest deposits of all were discovered and a veritable bonanza ensued. Blast furnaces were constructed at Beck Hole and later at Grosmont too. Men were brought in from as far afield as Norfolk and Cornwall to work in the mines and the associated installations which early photographic records show dominating the area around Grosmont. Ultimately, unable to compete with imported iron, the furnaces (now the car park!) shut down in 1891 and the mines themselves 24 years later.

But what of the railway? George Stephenson's original 24 mile (39km) track from Whitby to Pickering was opened on May 26th 1836, but in those early days carriages were scarcely more than stage-coaches mounted on bogies. In fact, passengers and freight were pulled along the line by horses for the first 11 years, until George Hudson introduced steam locomotives to expand his York and North Midland Railway.

Below: **Grosmont — northern terminus of the North York Moors Railway.**

Above: **'Dame Vera Lynn'** *leaving Grosmont.*

Right: **On the climb to Goathland in wooded Eller Beck gorge.**

Far right: **Above the Murk Esk in Crag Cliff Wood.**

For most of its outward leg, this walk follows Stephenson's railway trackbed—easy going as you might expect! It begins from a gate signposted 'Footpath to Goathland' at the level crossing and continues alongside viewing areas and over the Murk Esk by footbridge near its confluence with the River Esk. Soon you bear left up past the schoolroom and St Matthew's Church, founded in 1845 and 1842 respectively, though a larger church was built in 1875 to accommodate an expanding population. Down to your right, the smaller, turreted tunnel through which the original horse-drawn carriages passed was blasted through high ground, the deep river gorge here offering Stephenson no alternative. At its far end, visitors are able to view the Engine Shed which is equipped with a spectators' gallery.

Crossing the railway, our track climbs to an excellent vantage point above Grosmont and with binoculars you have a grandstand view of the station. A left turn leads through a handgate and downhill to an old North Eastern Railway trespass notice where the path runs alongside the modern track. A miscellany of ageing diesel locomotives and rolling stock acquired by the North York Moors Historical Railway Trust since its inauguration in 1967—some apparently beyond renovation—are lined up for the curious to gaze at: metal dinosaurs from another age of railway design!

Straight ahead, the working line diverges left to cross the Murk Esk, leaving the original track heading for the one-time miners' settlement of Esk Valley. Terraced cottages here were built to house workers in nearby whinstone and ironstone mines.

Meanders in the Murk Esk, drawing close to the track below Spring Wood, are crossed half a mile farther on by a steel footbridge resting on disproportionately massive stone piers that formerly supported the railway. A stile leads up into Blue Ber Wood, a delightful, well waymarked interlude—essentially a detour made necessary by floods in 1930 which washed away a bridge.

Emerging from the trees, the trackbed swings slowly left and crosses Eller Beck on giant stepping stones, the residual foundations of yet another bridge. (Should the beck be impassable here, steps are retraced about 50m and a path taken up to the road bridge in Beck Hole hamlet; a short distance to the right a path will be found rejoining the route.)

Beck Hole Station closed back in 1865 when a new line was pushed through to Goathland for steam locomotives, of which more in a moment. The rails from Grosmont, however, remained in situ and were briefly to see service 40 years later when autocars ran between here and Whitby during the years 1908 to 1914. If

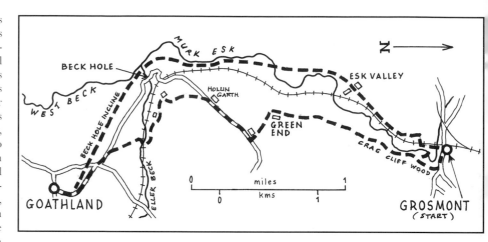

the time is right, there are few refreshment spots more pleasant than Beck Hole's village pub.

The 1 in 10 incline from Beck Hole to Goathland was a persistent headache to the early railway operators. Too steep for horses or locomotives to work, coaches and waggons had to be hauled up by rope (later by metal cable) and accidents inevitably occurred, culminating in a fatality in 1865. That same year, however, a 'Deviation Line' was blasted and bridged along the steep-sided Eller Beck valley at the then considerable cost of £50,000. In July the first steam loco passed through to Goathland and Beck Hole Incline was abandoned. Over a century was to pass before the infamous Dr Beeching axed the line south of Grosmont as part of his plan to rationalise Britain's railway network.

Today you would not recognise the onward way up to Goathland as belonging to a railway system unless you already knew. Trees and vegetation have narrowed the track to a woodland path, though the uphill slope remains, of course. In three-quarters of a mile (1.2km), you reach the road not far from Goathland village centre. In fact, the railway trail continues on to Goathland Station at the east side of the village and, if desired, you could catch a train back to Grosmont. Should a long wait be in prospect, Goathland's little refreshment places will satisfy the 'inner man' and even walkers intending to return to Grosmont on foot are recommended to break their journey here.

Heading back, you first make for the road at the Incline summit, turning right onto it and left at the crossroads. In about 250m, you cross a stile on the right into a narrow, hedged lane and follow it to a field, at the bottom edge of which steps descend towards the fast-flowing waters of Eller Beck. I have yet to discover a better viewpoint of trains labouring up the appreciable gradient to Goathland than the bank on the right. Walkers cross a footbridge directly beneath the railway bridge arch, so you have it all before you: woods, moorside, river, trail, bridges and trains!

Beyond Eller Beck, our path rises to another viewpoint at a bench, joins a track trending left above small Lins Farm and arrives opposite Hill Farm. Here you turn right, uphill, then left on a narrowing trod following a wall through bracken and over boggy ground; it takes you to the public road at Hollin Garth farmhouse. Five hundred metres north-east along the road, at a telephone box, you turn down left to Green End and at the bottom of the lane turn right along the farm track. This agricultural section continues down a grassy bank, crosses Crag Dikes footbridge and skirts the edge of Crag Cliff Wood, first to the right then through a corner to the left before entering the woods proper.

The walk's finale is a fitting one, for it adds unexpected dimensions in the form of splendid broad-leaved woodland and a fine stretch of exposed paved causeway.

Passing out of the wood, the paved way extends ahead to join a country lane. You turn left here through a gate and in about 50m it is well worth pausing to peer over a low bank on your left for a tree-shrouded but nevertheless exciting view of the Murk Esk flowing below an almost vertical drop of several hundred feet.

The simplest, most direct return to Grosmont uses a footbridge ahead—the lane drops to a ford and potentially wet feet for walkers! To reach the church up to the left is straightforward and brings you onto the outward path alongside the railway whose presence will in all probability have already been betrayed by the hiss of steam. If, however, you would like more woodland walking, you can watch for a path striking off to the right across a stream footbridge. Climbing delectably beneath a well established tree canopy, it gives out half way up the steep road hill opposite Park Villa, some 200m above Grosmont Station.

Facing page: **Leas Head Farm above the wooded Littlebeck Valley.**

WALK 18: *Falling Foss, Sneaton High Moor and May Beck*

Terrain: Fields, open moorland and wooded beckside paths. **Start/Finish:** Falling Foss car park (reached from Red Gate crossroads 2 miles (3km) south of Sneaton). **Distance:** 7 miles (11.2km)—allow 3½ to 4 hours. **Maps:** OS Landranger Sheet 94; Outdoor Leisure North-East sheet.

Becks draining north from Sneaton High Moor converge to form Little Beck which, in turn, joins the River Esk at Aislaby. So attractive is this valley with its mixed woodland, typical farmland and a beautiful waterfall, that two trails have been laid out, one around Falling Foss by the Forestry Commission, the other around May Beck by the National Park authorities. Both aim to help visitors appreciate the nature and management of the landscape and each has an accompanying leaflet obtainable from Information Centres.

Small parts of these trails are incorporated into this walk, but in total it casts a much wider net taking in Sneaton High Moor and the delightful, afforested May Beck valley. Should the weather be fine and you feel like extending the moorland section, a suggestion appears in the text which adds about 3 miles (5km) and takes you past further ancient sites.

There is a good-sized car park at Falling Foss (Map Ref: 888 036), for walkers and non-walkers alike come here to admire the 30ft (9m) waterfall set in its pretty, wooded ravine. My own preferred season for the walk is springtime, when leaves are vibrant green and wild flowers are blooming. Early autumn is equally attractive—moorland heather and bracken are at their most colourful—but high summer, despite the obvious advantages of long daylight hours and

holidays, fills the valley with lush vegetation and insects are more numerous.

You start from the car park by walking down the track to railings overlooking the cascade—a magnificent sight after heavy rain—and crossing the footbridge to Midge Hall. On still summer evenings the reason for its unusual name becomes painfully apparent! This is the old Keeper's Cottage to Newton House which stands 500m up to the north; built in the late 1700s as a shooting lodge, it was converted to an Outdoor Activities Centre in 1967.

For 50m you walk along the west bank of May Beck, then turn right up a broad farm track at the forest boundary. Views, hitherto contained within the canopy of woodland, begin to open out as you pass to the left of Foss Farm barns. Beyond a left-hand bend you turn right through a gate onto a pleasantly undulating field track which crosses Parsley Beck just downstream of a small lake. Leas Head Farm, duckpond and all, is negotiated by cutting sharp left up a stony track and for the first time there are distant views to the sea between a shallow fold of hills.

The bridleway you are now walking up—the old Leas Head Road—skirts field tops, forking towards Grosmont at the next gate as an ancient route over Sleights Moor past High and Low Bridestones. For the time being, prospects over to the east are almost archetypically pastoral, but after crossing rough grazing you emerge into the bracken of Sheep House Rigg.

Contouring at first over rough slopes parallel to Parsley Beck and the impenetrable edge of Newton House Plantation, a little height is gained through heather towards the moortop, where man's presence is marked by pylons and distant traffic on the A169. Eventually the path trends left to cross the head of Parsley Beck near the plantation corner and from here our route continues in a south-westerly direction over rugged heather moor. In poor visibility, a line of posts would indicate the way and you pass beneath the high tension power cables.

Throughout the modest ascent just completed, a corresponding transition has occurred in your surroundings. Improved farmland at lower levels is drained using underground pipes and is regularly manured to yield grass and arable crops: the breeding and rearing of livestock is central to the local agricultural economy. At intermediate levels, rough pasture is really only enclosed moorland, improved in the sense that controlled grazing has modified the

Above: **The boundary stones on Sheephouse Rigg.**

Below: **Overgrown quarry workings on the Whinstone Ridge.**

Facing page: **Lovely May Beck on its course downstream towards Falling Foss waterfall.**

natural vegetation. Open moor remains largely untouched save for the periodic burning of heather and some drainage of wetter areas. It is characterised by extensive heather and ling, bracken, rushes and rough indigenous grasses, though there were times—before Bronze Age man—when the moors were covered with light forests of oak, elm, alder, birch, lime, ash, hazel and willow.

At the final rising edge of moor appear two boundary stones. Their inscriptions, eroded by 200 years of wind, rain and frost, are not too distinct, but York Assizes figures clearly and the taller stone is dated 1784. They stand beside a broad, rutted trackway following the line of the Whinstone Ridge which stretches, ruler-straight, north-west to south-east from Esk Dale to Fylingdales Moors. Sometimes referred to as the Cleveland Dyke, this intrusion of basalt—a lava flow from 58 million years ago—has been extensively quarried for roadstone. Here and there along its length, disused workings form elongated trenches where the hard rock was extracted.

Heading south-east, the track draws closer to the edge of Newton House Plantation and in 500m reaches the brow of York Cross Rigg at a junction. This itinerary, choosing the delightful descent of May Beck, continues straight ahead, but a longer loop could be made taking in Ann's Cross, Louven Howe and John Cross. If opted for, you branch right up past Foster Howes and Ann's Cross and on to Louven Howe. At the post and cairn—not far north from Lilla Howe and the North York Moors' oldest cross, well worth a detour—you veer north-east on a less distinct and rather boggy path shadowing the plantation boundary to the two standing stones called Old Wife's Neck. From there via John Cross it is all downhill to May Beck car park where you resume the described walk, which now continues.

About 300m beyond the track junction on the Whinstone Ridge, you come upon the stump of York (or Jack) Cross in its stone socket. Though no longer a major landmark, it is situated at an intersection between the old sea or town road and Abbey road, the latter evidently a once busy thoroughfare judging by its size. During its heyday as an Abbey and small port, Whitby had no other means of communicating south and west overland except by packhorse ways over the moors. York Cross, so named perhaps because of its position on the Whitby to York road, was almost certainly erected as a guide post.

Ahead, the track drops towards Newton House Plantation, disused whinstone quarries on Pike Hill unplanted by the Forestry Commission. Since 1921 they have planted almost 50,000 acres of forest in the North York Moors

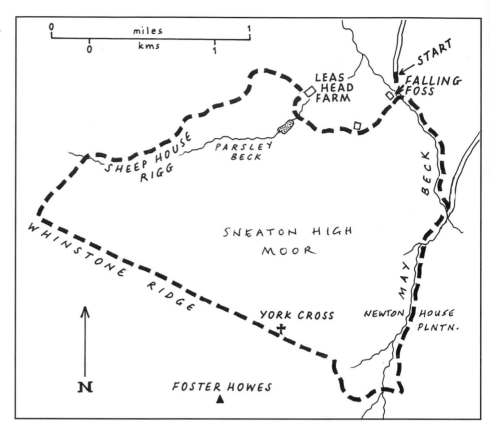

region, mainly in the south and east. Sneaton High Moor's mantle of conifers (North American Lodgepole Pine, Sitka Spruce, Larch and Scots Pine are the principal species used on these poor upland soils) represents the last major afforestation scheme and dates from 1968.

You go down a broad ride into the plantation and at the forestry road turn right. Forking left at the next junction takes you over May Beck and up past a pond; in 100m you strike off left down a ride and left again on a clear track. Very soon surroundings open out above May Beck's overgrown little valley and you are descending an attractive path to stream level. The beck's waters babble quietly over rock steps beneath shady banks; lower down where the valley steepens, a gate and stile herald the plantation's perimeter. The beck is crossed near miniature waterfalls, heard but not seen in summer's profuse growth, and at the top of the following abrupt slope a right turn is taken down to the Forestry Commission's May Beck car park and picnic area.

In fine weather during the holiday season this is a favourite spot for families, as well as being the starting point for a Farm Trail and riverside walks. We, too, turn downstream across the road bridge and immediately left by a red waymark post. Well walked, the trail crosses grassy levels and climbs beneath old oak trees. Attempts to stock May Beck with fish have not met with

success: Falling Foss waterfall and the mill dam at Littlebeck have always prevented natural colonisation and it is thought that insufficient sources of food account for the inability of artificially introduced fish to survive.

Wider now, May Beck meanders along its rocky bed flanked by deciduous woods. Near a large cluster of blackthorn, you pass a muddy pond originally created with the intention of attracting frogs, toads and newts whose natural habitats are being progressively lost to contamination and drainage schemes.

Provided you are not undertaking the walk in wet weather when the beck is in spate, it is possible, by keeping left at a path fork, to cross the water on boulders at a shallow bend. This provides a scenic return to Midge Hall and thence over the footbridge back to the car park. Following heavy rain, however, you might need to fork right on the upper path leading back through woods of Scots Pine and European Larch planted 50 years ago.

Facing page: **Looking back round Robin Hood's Bay from the clifftops at Ravenscar.**

WALK 19: *Robin Hood's Bay to Ravenscar*

Terrain: Well walked cliff and field paths with a few steep gradients; easy railway trackbed walking to return. **Start/Finish:** Robin Hood's Bay village. **Distance:** 9 miles (15km)—including Geological Trail. **Maps:** OS Landranger Sheet 94; Outdoor Leisure North-East sheet.

Even including a return along the old Yorkshire coast railway trackbed, this route is not especially long. With suitable transport it could be walked in one direction, or the loop shortened at any one of several points. For such a compact stretch of coast, there is a surprising concentration of historical and geological interest.

Despite its name, Robin Hood's Bay has no apparent connections with the famous outlaw of Sherwood Forest. Indeed, right up until the early sixteenth century, threatened attack by Danish raiders had deterred coastal settlement, but by 1538 a community of fifty houses had developed. Initially, Bay (or Bay Town) as it is known locally, comprised the inhabitants of nearby Raw who had moved to the shoreline for the fishing. As increasing wealth was generated from this and merchant shipping, so the village expanded, until by the nineteenth century it had eclipsed Whitby as a fishing port. More than 130 local fishermen sailing 40 cobles and 5 larger herring craft supported a thriving community; everyone was involved, whether helping to pull up the boats, mending nets, baiting lines, making lobster pots or barrelling fish for market.

In 1885 the railway came and with it new markets for fish and the beginnings of tourism. Mount Pleasant was developed on high ground near the railway station, home to retired sea captains, shipowners and professional people, but at about the same time fishing here was declining due to lack of proper harbour facilities for the larger vessels then evolving. By the 1920s, only a handful of fishermen remained in work, though today there are signs of a revival.

Smuggling in Bay was rife and contraband could be passed right up the village, so the story goes, through a network of passages and false-backed cupboards connecting the houses and pubs! Many dwellings still show signs of their seafaring associations: nautical motifs, ships' names, mementoes in gardens. The railway closed in 1965 but Bay continues to attract visitors in large numbers. As one might expect, there are shops, pubs and eating places, as well as an interesting little museum. In my view, the place is not at its best on overcrowded summer days, though few people stray far along the coast path.

Cars must be parked at the top of Bay Bank where stands a memorial to the rescue of the brig *Visitor* in 1981. Walking starts steeply downhill to The Dock, traditional hub of village life where you will still find cobles and lobster pots and the old lifeboat shelter.

Although the route itself starts from a 'Cliff Path' sign in Albion Street, a good look at the foreshore and paved slipway is always rewarding. At high tide, especially if a swell is running, the sea's all-pervading presence can seem menacing and little imagination is required to invoke images of its destructive power. In 1780 a major cliff fall took away much of King Street—hitherto the village's main thoroughfare—including two rows of cottages. Storms and subsidence of the soft boulder clay have claimed some two hundred dwellings over the past two centuries; even the massive concrete sea wall constructed in 1975 will need constant maintenance if it, too, is not to succumb.

At low tide, wave-cut platforms of impure limestone within the Lower Lias extend out 600m in curving 'scars' and are a striking feature of this coast for 3 miles (4.5km) to the southeast. Fishermen utilise the shelter provided by these reefs but they are also a favourite haunt of fossil-seekers and rock-pool explorers. Provided you are sure not to get cut off by a rising tide, it is possible to reach our first destination—Boggle Hole—by walking along the beach.

At the end of Albion Street, Flagstaff Steps lead up to timber duckboarding, though you could, if particularly interested, detour first of all to Marnar Dale Wildflower Reserve by keeping right. Between bushes and trees beside the coast path, fine views open out back over the pantiled huddle of Robin Hood's Bay and the high, eroding cliffs reaching out to Ness Point (or North Cheek).

A long-distance hiker walks duck-boarding over eroding cliffs near Robin Hood's Bay.

Timber walkways have been installed where the path has slipped away in the vicinity of Farsyde Stud and Riding Centre. Erosion on the Yorkshire coast is a serious problem and it is estimated that, on average, 2in. (5cm) each year are lost to the sea: 20in. (50cm) every decade. In 500m you drop steeply into the wooded ravine of Mill Beck; Boggle Hole youth hostel and Field Centre used to be Bay's water-powered corn mill, rebuilt after serious flood damage in 1857. Its intriguing name derives from the Yorkshire term 'boggle' for a hobgoblin or sprite who, if treated well enough, would offer various magic cures.

After crossing the footbridge and turning inland up the lane for a few metres, you reach a flight of steps on the left signed 'Cleveland Way'; this well known long-distance footpath runs through the National Park and down the coast from Saltburn to Filey Brigg. A stiff little climb ensues to regain clifftop level, but in no time at all you are descending steeply again to the footbridge over Stoupe Beck, with magnificent views of the cliffs ahead at Ravenscar.

Paving slabs by a very muddy bridleway climb to Stoupe Bank Farm and a tarmac lane where, just short of Stoupebrow Cottage Farm, a continuation of the coast path is waymarked along the undulating seaward edge of fields. You pass a World War II bunker at Peter White Cliff, still walking above spectacular low-tide scars, until stiles lead you inland over fields.

Being so well used, the way ahead is quite clear; however, where it swings right, uphill by trees, you take the left fork which crosses a stream between cattle grids and veers up across golf links towards the cliff line. There are splendid prospects back round the arc of Robin Hood's Bay to its tightly-clustered, sea-walled village.

A signposted and steep footpath to the shore forms part of a Geological Trail, a booklet to accompany which can be purchased at the National Trust Information Centre a little way up from the car park. South Cheek headland is protected by a prominent reef of resistant, Middle Lias rock associated with the great Peak Fault which runs seaward as a well defined edge. Muds and silts laid down on a seabed in the Jurassic Period around 160 million years ago were compressed and tilted into the strata of sedimentary rocks visible today. Down at beach level, skeletons of small creatures are preserved as fossils—notably ammonites, oysters and belemnites—while many of the pebbles and boulders are 'erratics' carried here by receding glaciers during the last Ice Age. Walking beneath these high, slumped cliffs and out onto the foreshore scars at low tide is an experience guaranteed to stimulate an interest in geology if it did not already exist!

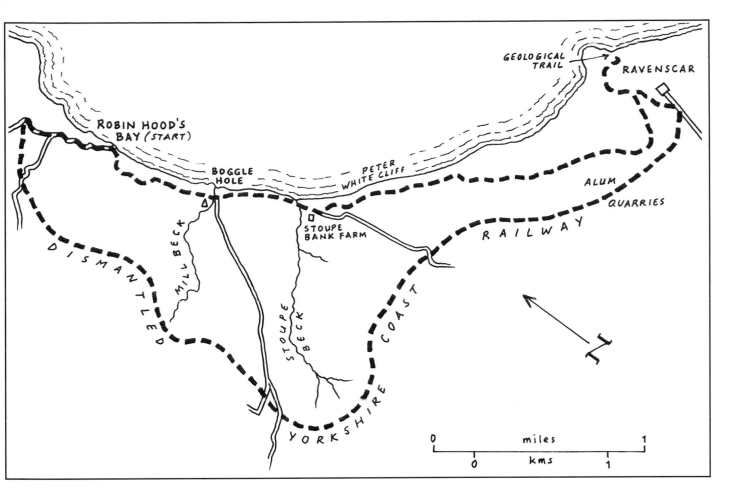

More than 600ft (180m) of concerted ascent is involved to reach Ravenscar; near the top you will pass below the castellated walls of the Raven Hall Hotel where weary Lyke Wake Walk participants hobble in for a celebratory drink! The rather grandiose building began life as a private residence, built on the site of a Roman signal station in 1774. George III spent many periods of time here being treated for 'madness'—that most imprecise of terms—to which he finally succumbed in 1811.

Ravenscar village, such as it is, lies half a mile up the road. Had the local geology proved more stable, development of holiday accommodation and amenities might have been extensive, though whether the prospective resort would ever have rivalled Scarborough as some hoped is open to question. One's impressions today are of an oddly incomplete place, heightened by its proximity to the dismantled coast railway which once brought trippers and the promise of prosperity.

Our return itinerary—at first part of the Geological Trail—begins from the National Trust Centre. You gain access to the old railway trackbed by turning left a few metres beyond a white, five-bar gate and soon approach dis-

used alum quarries. Between the seventeenth and nineteenth centuries, alum was employed widely as a fixing agent for textile dyes, in paper-making and to cure animal hides. Quarried shale contained about 2 per cent mineral alum and a lengthy process was entailed to obtain a usable product. The shale was fired with brushwood, mixed with water, concentrated by boiling and mixed with an alkali—usually urine shipped here by the barrel-load from London pubs! Alum crystals formed when the solution cooled but this method of production ended when a cheaper alternative source was discovered using colliery waste. Ravenscar's alum quarry closed down in 1862, becoming, fifty years later, the site of a brickworks whose kilns and railway sidings, though largely disintegrated, are still discernible. Wild flowers and shrubs have colonised the banks, while here and there subsidence interrupts the surface, graphically illustrating the area's unreliable geology.

The 21 miles (34km) of line linking Scarborough with Whitby was engineered by John Waddell and the service opened in 1885. One of England's most scenic railways, it was served by 8 stations, the highest being Ravenscar where trains entered a tunnel at 631ft (192m) above sea

level. In company with many of our country branch lines, it was closed by Dr Beeching in 1965; although not a definitive right-of-way, the dismantled trackbed has been designated a 'Permitted Path'.

After passing beneath the road at Stoupe Brow and skirting close to Browside Farm, the trackbed circumvents the valley of Stoupe Beck in a wide, inland loop. You are walking atop embankments at Allison Head Wood, then crossing two arms of Bridge Holm Lane leading to Boggle Hole, the first by bridge, the second by steps. A picnic area near the erstwhile halt is followed by an inhabited cottage and, at one point, an arch of alder trees. Trending seaward again, progress is perfectly straightforward, descending over Middlewood Lane, passing a caravan site and growing perceptibly more pastoral as Fylingthorpe is approached. Once over King's Beck, you turn right onto the Robin Hood's Bay road, pass the church and arrive back at the top car park.

WALK 20: *Simon Howe, Wade's Causeway and Mallyan Spout*

Terrain: Everything from exposed moorland to stony tracks, country road and a scrambly ravine. **Start/Finish:** The Mallyan Hotel, Goathland.
Distance: 9½ miles (15km)—allow 4 to 5 hours. **Maps:** OS Landranger Sheet 94; Outdoor Leisure South-East sheet.

There is a generosity of space at Goathland that seems to absorb visitors, no matter how many make demands upon it. Held between West Beck and Eller Beck, the upper village has spread around open common, grazed to the cottage doors by sheep. The war memorial is a replica of the 1300 year-old Lilla Cross on Fylingdales Moor, one of England's oldest Christian monuments.

Goathland's popularity is well deserved, for not only does the North York Moors steam railway between Grosmont and Pickering stop here—a prodigious attraction in its own right during the operating periods—but the surrounding country offers walks of varying length through magnificent landscapes. You will find a range of accommodation and refreshment places in the village, so it would make a good base for exploring the eastern moors and dales; it is also, of course, no distance from the coast.

Many come here to hike the Historical Railway Trail to Grosmont (see Walk 17) and to catch a steam-hauled train back. However, our eyes are fixed firmly on rising moorland to the south and, from the road junction opposite the Mallyan Hotel, a grassy path slopes up past a bench, angling away from the road. One or two other paths penetrate the bracken and rights-of-way marked on the Outdoor Leisure sheet can be misleading; you keep straight on, veering south and aiming for the highest visible ground.

Over a rise, The Tarn hoves into sight on the right and our by now rather indistinct bridleway reaches a ruin near the shore—Old Kit Bield. 'Bields' are dry-stone walled enclosures put up as protection for sheep against harsh winter weather that often afflicts these moors. Walkers, too, are not averse to using them on stormy days!

A green hatched right-of-way on the 1:25,000 map is drawn turning up left (south) here and a thin trod does, indeed, branch off through the heather to Two Howes. Closer inspection of the map will also reveal the black hatched line of an actual track continuing along The Tarn's southern bank before striking up by its feeder stream. Both paths are walkable, but the inconsistency highlights the dilemma faced by walkers when, for instance, a map right-of-way does not exist on the ground, or else an obvious pathway is not given right-of-way status. When in doubt, experienced walkers will rely on their best judgement at the time, but it is worth remembering that over three-quarters of the National

Park is in private ownership and that abuse of access concessions only gives walkers a bad name and can even contribute to erosion of fragile moorland vegetation.

So much for technicalities! Both paths converge near Two Howes, twin mounds topped by cairns. 'Howes' (or barrows) such as these—and there are more than 3000 of them dotted over the North York Moors—are the last resting places of important people from the Middle Bronze Age. Their distinctive silhouettes usually crown ridges or watersheds so that, on horizons as long and as lacking in distinctive features as these, they become recognisable landmarks. In steeper, more broken country, you would scarcely notice them at all.

Sad to say, the majority of howes were ransacked a century ago for whatever treasures they contained and sold to respectable Victorian collectors for whom the acquisition of such rare objects was all the rage. They and their grave-robbing accomplices were equally culpable and with no records being kept of what came from where, much valuable material was lost forever. A few howes escaped intact and have provided archaeologists with important data on burial customs of the time. Before leaving, you might catch a glimpse of the Fylingdales Early Warning Station 'golf balls': 2000 years of history in one view!

You pass close to the westernmost howe and in 200m fork left. Now the well walked, peaty path stays on the broad whaleback of Two Howes Rigg and is marked by the occasional cairn. With rising ground soon close ahead, you keep right at a path junction and climb the last

few metres to Simon Howe. It is a high point of some significance, for in addition to the OS pillar over to the north-east at 853ft (260m) above sea level, the large cairn nearer at hand is surrounded by a ring of small standing stones.

Even in the worst visibility, deep snow cover excepted, you will be impressed—appalled perhaps—by the eroded scar of a path bisecting the moor from east to west. The challenge of the Lyke Wake Walk has been met by countless thousands of walkers over the 35 years since its inauguration by Bill Cowley. Individuals and groups alike from all walks of life have set out to tramp the 40 miles (64km) from Scarth Wood Moor to Ravenscar within the 24 hours time limit. Whether you are successful or not seems less important than taking part, and the route's popularity has been astonishing. However, what lies before you is the result!

In common with many paths crossing vulnerable terrain, heavy usage causes the main trod to become too deeply rutted for walking comfort. It collects water, too, and is eventually ignored as flanking paths are established. So seriously is the problem being taken along parts of the Lyke Wake Walk that the National Park authorities are advising larger groups to choose alternative challenge routes such as the Shepherd's Round.

Turning west, you follow the path alongside Howl Moor Dike stream for a while before its bed swings off left. Within 15 minutes Hunt House Crag is reached—the eastern rim of Wheeldale and well worth pausing at for the view over Wheeldale Beck and Wheeldale

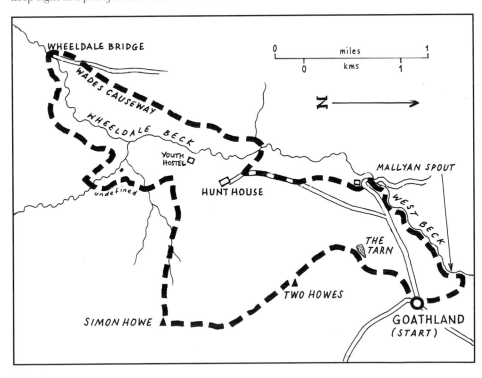

Lodge youth hostel. Our return leg traces the nearer skyline from left to right.

A few metres downhill, you take a track left which climbs back to the moor edge and contours left through the heather. It is double-rutted, a sure sign of occasional use by Land Rover, and heads for the upper corner of forest on Gale Hill Rigg. Unfortunately, after bending right towards an old nissen hut and ruined shepherd's shelter (John O' Groats' on the map), it peters out! There is really no need for compass work unless you are completely disorientated in mist—you simply bear left along the top edge of bracken above Blawath Beck then angle down towards a stile into the plantation next to a conspicuous rock slab. You cross the beck here and once in the trees walk up the narrow ride and turn right onto a forestry track.

Further on, a broad gravel road downhill takes you round Gale Hill Point and in about a mile deposits you in the open at Wheeldale Bridge. You may be surprised to see cars and people here, though they are not usually present in any numbers. A narrow moor road, often closed in a snowy winter, makes a beeline from Egton Bridge to Pickering but its tarmac surface gives way to dirt here and only those motorists with sporting pretensions and a disregard for their tyres continue over Ramsden Head to Mauley Cross in Cropton Forest and thence via Newton-on-Rawcliffe to Pickering.

Having crossed the metal footbridge over Wheeldale Beck, you walk for a short distance alongside Sod Fold Slack and cross it too. Ahead lies one of Britain's best preserved stretches of original Roman road. It runs north-east from Cawthorn Camp, part of a road connecting the fort at Malton with Whitby and the coastal signal stations, though no traces of it have been found beyond the Esk valley. Clearly visible are the embankment, upon which rough sandstone slabs were laid, and the side drains necessary to take away excess rainwater. When in use by Roman legionnaires, a top dressing of small stones and gravel would have been pressed into the remaining gaps.

In the interests of posterity and comfortable walking it is probably best to proceed alongside the actual roadway which is now unevenly paved and rises a foot or so above level ground. Although in the custody of the Department of the Environment, Wade's Causeway belongs to HM Queen Elizabeth, through the Duchy of Lancaster. The sheer audacity of roadbuilding across such inhospitable moorland can be appreciated by glancing west to the wilderness of Wheeldale Moor whose farthest horizons are only given scale by a distant fringe of conifers, a north-thrusting finger of Cropton Forest.

Altogether there is nearly a mile of excavated Roman road, though its line is clear for 5 miles (8km) from Cawthorn over the Pickering and Wheeldale moors. You will soon encounter the Lyke Wake path for a second time. It comes in from the west—a walkers' highway in a desert of windswept heather—crosses the tarmacked Wheeldale Road and drops to stepping stones over Wheeldale Beck near the youth hostel. From there, a handy short-cut back to Goathland, if one is needed, passes Hunt House and follows Hunt House Lane back to the starting point. More entertainingly, this route continues forward through gates along by a field wall and down a grassy bank past two trees to Hazel Head Woods at the confluence of Wheeldale Gill and Wheeldale Beck to form West Beck.

Here you cross the footbridge and turn sharp right, climbing out to meet the metalled Hunt House Road at parking spaces. Only 500m north along the tarmac, just before the road bends right, you fork down left on a clear grassy track through bracken. At a gate you veer right, though a left turn will deliver you quickly to Nelly Ayre Foss; with Water Arc Foss, Thomason Foss and Mallyan Spout, it is one of a series of waterfalls in the locality.

Red-roofed New Wath House ahead precedes arrival at the minor road between Goathland and Egton Bridge. Below a sharp bend, a white fence just before the road bridge is your key to finding the final exhilarating section of this walk. Though signed, the footpath entrance is narrow, leading you into the dramatic recesses of West Beck gorge. If the beck is in spate I would not guarantee you a dry or even a viable passage, but in normal conditions the way is merely tortuous.

Several such gorges exist in the region—steep-sided, rocky ravines which contain fast-flowing, bouldery streams, waterfalls and inaccessible woods. Progress on the scrambly, switchback path can be slow, especially in wet weather when already rounded rocks at the beckside beneath New Wath Scar become treacherously slippery. Once a stile is passed, however, most of the ankle-twisting terrain is behind you and the path levels off through trees. One tricky section remains where the path is forced high to negoti-

Left: ***Fylingdales Early Warning Station from Simon Howe.***

Facing page: ***Wade's Causeway — a marvellous excavated section of old Roman road running across Wheeldale Moor.***

ate a landslip; at the time of writing the path is still falling away and may need to be re-routed yet again.

Quite suddenly the 76ft (23m) plume of Mallyan Spout appears ahead, cascading over a rocky lip into the wooded ravine. During dry spells the volume of water quickly diminishes to a disappointing trickle as the area of land it drains is relatively small; at such times there are plentiful opportunities for boulder-hopping in the stream bed by way of compensation! After heavy rain, the waterfall assumes a more aggressive character and you are unlikely to pass it without a wetting. In fact, you can dodge right behind the cascade and, after a little more rocky walking, arrive at a waymarking signpost.

Mallyan Spout is a major summer attraction so the path up right beside a belt of pine trees to the Mallyan Hotel is well used; in a few hundred metres you have returned to the walk's starting point.

WALK 21: *Cloughton and Hayburn Wykes by the Coast Path*

Terrain: Undulating, eroding clifftops, woodland paths and an old railway trackbed. **Start/Finish:** Cloughton Wyke car park. **Distance:** 6 miles (9.5km)—allow 3 to 4 hours. **Maps:** OS Landranger Sheets 94 and 101; Outdoor Leisure South-East sheet.

South of Robin Hood's Bay the coast takes on a quite different character from the stark headlands and rock-scarred foreshore further northwest. Here, for the most part, cliffs are noticeably stepped, each 'tread' bearing the debris of old rock-falls heavily colonised by vegetation. A lack of stream valleys combined with a protective skirt of large sandstone boulders acting as breakwaters have left the cliff line intact and, apart from the two 'wykes' (Yorkshire for small sheltered inlets) we are about to explore, there are no bays as such between Ravenscar and Scarborough.

Trees and plants grow profusely in places, lending an air of warm luxuriance to parts of the walk. Nevertheless, there is open clifftop too and should the weather be windy or wet you will need to tread carefully wherever the path draws close to the crumbling edge far above the waves.

As it stands, the walk is a circular one, but with two cars, or an obliging non-walker willing to drop you off and collect you, it could be walked in one direction as a pleasant 2 hour coastal jaunt. The return leg is along the dismantled Yorkshire Coast Railway trackbed which time and nature have transformed into an almost woodland route.

Cloughton stands 4 miles (6.5km) north of Scarborough on the A171. From the village centre a metalled lane to the right can be found heading for the coast; it crosses the dismantled railway and at the road end is a small car park overlooking Cloughton Wyke, a haunt of sea-anglers. Steps take you down to the coast path which immediately provides a definitive view of this attractive little bay—a much more accessible and public one than Hayburn Wyke which can only be reached on foot.

On the 1:25,000 map, the miniature inlet appears as Salt Pans—a reference no doubt to the days when sea water was evaporated to form salt, a vital commodity before the advent of refrigeration and one upon which fishing communities relied to preserve their catch. The onward path undulates along with views inland of a valley parallel to the coast through which the old railway once ran.

Soon there are steep steps to climb flanking a wood: if you pause at the top to catch your breath, be sure to glance back towards the defi-

ant bulk of Scarborough Castle in the distance. Particularly in summer, it is not always possible to look down on sea and foreshore thanks to a screen of low trees and bushes, amongst which you will find sessile oak, hawthorn and blackthorn, elderberry, gorse and blackberry. Even in winter there is a sufficient density of branches to take the sting out of a bullying wind!

High, now, above overgrown undercliff and warm-hued boulders, your way is hemmed in between agricultural land and a far from secure cliff edge. Jealously exploiting their disappearing fields to the full, some farmers seem to plough or fence with scant regard for the poor hiker, who is forced to run the gauntlet of potential catastrophe. To experienced coastal walkers it is a familiar enough situation and danger may be more imagined than real. That said, someone somewhere will be in the wrong place at the wrong time, with possibly fatal consequences. I well recall as narrow an escape as one cares to contemplate when the cliff path collapsed directly ahead of my feet while walking the North Cornwall coast: it disappeared like a descending lift and had I arrived there 10 seconds earlier you would certainly not be reading this! But that is another story. It all boils down to

being 'coastwise'—keeping as well back from big drops as you can and taking no unnecessary risks, especially in stormy weather when wind and rain conspire to de-stabilise the exposed cliff face.

Past Rodger Trod and Iron Scar, the densely vegetated Little Cliff stretches below and in the vicinity of Tindall Point there are marvellous open views ahead down to Hayburn Wyke's diminutive beach. A right turn is made and you are descending quite steeply through woods; in late springtime the pathside is ablaze with bluebells, anemones and celandines.

You are entering the Yorkshire Naturalists' Trust Nature Reserve created to protect the habitats of many beautiful flowers, including wild honeysuckle, common spotted orchids, lady's mantle and enchanter's nightshade, as well as several bird species and the woodland itself. Stepped in places, the path weaves down to a footbridge over Hayburn Beck, but instead of crossing it you walk right to emerge on a rocky platform above a waterfall.

Of all the delightful spots on this outing, here is one to savour! Easy scrambling to the right takes you onto the beach, an ankle-twisting expanse of pale, rounded pebbles interspersed

Facing page: **Near Cloughton Wyke at the start of the walk.**

Right: **Hayburn Wyke from the cliffs at Tindall Point.**

Above: **The little waterfall at Hayburn Wyke.**

Facing page: **Whisper Dales — an intimate, pastoral landscape surrounded by wooded hills.**

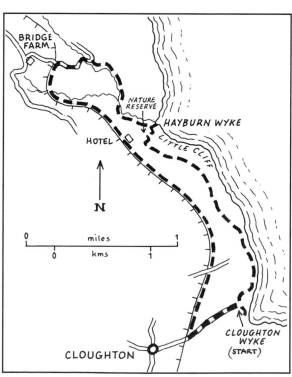

with rocks and boulders. From this angle the cascade is seen to best effect and is impressive, for its size, after heavy rain. Successive visits tend to underline the essential instability of natural land forms.

Returning to the path behind the waterfall, you climb back up steps to the Nature Reserve sign and Cleveland Way post (the final section of this long-distance route passes down the coast from Saltburn to Filey Brigg). A broad footpath to the right is now taken, followed shortly by a right fork which will lead you along above the beck and across its ravine on an airy little footbridge.

Public access to these lovely deciduous woods—mostly oak with ash, hazel and hawthorn—is unrestricted, but the Yorkshire Naturalists' Trust are anxious that people should never pick flowers, trample plant life off the paths, or damage the trees and rocks. It is all a matter of trust and the reserve's saving grace must be its inaccessibility by car: vandals don't generally like venturing too far off the beaten track!

Hayburn Beck flows prettily between mossy boulders in an intimate, deeply wooded valley. It may not be typical, but I have only ever encountered two other walkers during several visits here and I remember the half mile or so of secretive, enclosed stillness with great affection.

Undulations in the knobbly path give way to more concerted ascent and you surface at a handgate by a sign 'To Beach and Cliff'. After crossing a small field on the public bridleway, you turn left down the country lane opposite a bungalow, staying on it over a tributary of Hayburn Beck and up past Lowfield camp site. The lane soon reaches a bridge spanning the old railway trackbed which is joined here for the walk's return leg.

You might expect a railway track to provide easy going for hikers—which it does—but it may come as a surprise to discover the wayside shaded by a fringe of birch, scrub willow and other flora, in places almost forming a woodland corridor. Once one of Britain's most scenic lines, the Whitby to Scarborough Railway is now just a cinder track—a 'Permitted Path' (though not a definitive right-of-way) which gives you about $2\frac{1}{2}$ miles (4km) of straightforward southerly progress past farmland and woods.

At first it makes a big loop round Hayburn Beck then, beyond the Hayburn Wyke Hotel, ducks into a mile-long valley which cuts off sea views but provides variety which, after all, is as much the spice of walking as it is of life! When you are approaching Court Green Farm and the outskirts of Cloughton village, it is time to leave the trackbed and tramp the remaining half mile seaward to the car park at Cloughton Wyke.

WALK 22: *Whisper Dales, Broxa Forest and the River Derwent*

Terrain: Field paths and forest tracks, wet underfoot in places. One moderate climb. **Start/Finish:** Reasty Bank Forestry Commission car park. **Distance:** 8 miles (13km)—allow 4 to 5 hours. **Maps:** OS Landranger Sheets 94 and 101; Outdoor Leisure South-East sheet.

Reasty Bank is situated due south of Robin Hood's Bay and due west of Cloughton, not far from the village of Harwood Dale. At the bank top, on the Scalby to Harwood Dale 'B' road, the Forestry Commission has laid out a car park and picnic area.

West and south from here stretch vast tracts of mostly conifer forest. In addition to numerous waymarked trails, forest drives, nature walks and picnic sites, there are miles of rough roads, rides and pathways along which you can wander in peace and solitude. Once off the beaten track, a large scale map and a compass will often be necessary to avoid becoming disorientated and even totally lost!

Tramping all day through the heart of pine forest, however, may not be your favourite pastime: it certainly isn't mine! Views are restricted and on either side of the path lies a dark, impenetrable world of crowded trees. That said, walks which incorporate sections of forest do provide variety and in small doses the silent mystery of so much untrodden ground seems intriguing. In rough weather, forest walking is deliciously sheltered.

Although not visited by the following itinerary, I would recommend a trip to the Forestry Commission's Centre at Low Dalby, reached by toll road north from Thornton Dale or southwest from Langdale End. The forestry village there, built in 1949, has been augmented by a Visitor Centre and forestry offices housed in converted farm buildings and forms an excellent base from which to explore Dalby Forest.

Short, colour-coded, waymarked trails abound, mostly between 1 and 3 miles (1.5 and 5km) in length and not of 'classic walk' stature but nevertheless offering pleasant, informative strolls in the adjacent forest. The Visitor Centre contains exhibitions of wildlife and the Forestry Commission's work, as well as books, leaflets, maps and souvenirs for sale. Refreshment kiosk, drinking water, toilets, telephone and generous car parking space complete an amenity of considerable charm.

From the car park on Reasty Bank, you set off walking south-west down a gravelly road. (It is important to start in the correct direction, for other rough roads could send you astray before you have begun!) In 500m or so, having passed innumerable picnic spots, the track veers left and starts to lose height down Swinesgill Rigg. At my last visit, banksides were seriously eroding and trees in imminent danger of collapse, though presumably the Forestry Commission will take appropriate action before they fall.

Soon you emerge from forest into the open above Whisperdales Farm, a cluster of low buildings set in an intimate, pastoral landscape surrounded by wooded hills. Beyond the farm entrance you continue ahead to the right of Whisperdales Beck under a bank. The field track runs alongside the stream before crossing it and rising slightly onto a raised ledge between fields. Reaching a stile by Breaday Gill, you proceed ahead over grass, with Haggland Wood above you on the left.

While many places leave us guessing as to how they acquired their map names, Whisper Dales fulfils its promise as a haven of peaceful seclusion. There is a soft and rounded gentleness to its character, a sense of aloofness from the modern world through being passed by more often than visited.

Over more stiles, the way leads through meadows and past hawthorn trees to Lowdales Farm. Here you cross two shallow fords by a footbridge—indeed, the entire lane can turn into a ford after heavy rain—and keep left at a farm road junction. Just before the next footbridge over Lowdales Beck, by a bridleway sign on the left, you turn right up an ancient 'hollow way' worn into a sunken groove by centuries of use. Today only the occasional passing walker is seen and low, overhanging trees form a tunnel of foliage. When more open woodland is reached, you keep straight ahead; paved in places, the old way climbs to the head of a small valley and continues between hedges to a gate in the corner of Broxa Farm.

Turning right alongside the farm complex you reach a road junction. Tiny Broxa hamlet lies to the left—on this occasion only of possible interest for its telephone box—but the onward route turns right along a poorly surfaced lane towards the line of forest ahead.

At the edge of trees, you strike off left past a pole barrier on a path skirting the forest. The first track you come to on the right would offer an easy return short-cut, avoiding the descent into the Derwent valley and the subsequent climb out; in about $1\frac{1}{2}$ miles (2.5km) you would arrive at Barns Cliff End where the main route is rejoined.

The path soon swings right, taking you downhill on a gentle gradient through delightful broadleaved woods above Lang Dale. Eventu-

Left: **Walkers in Whisper Dales, Swinesgill Rigg in the background.**

Facing page: **Low North Camp from the forestry road on Reasty Bank.**

ally you turn right onto a riverside path which has followed the meandering Derwent north from Langdale End. Beyond a footbridge and marker post the walking becomes shady and secretive, twisting through mixed forest, a little boggy here and there but thoroughly entertaining. With the nearest public road a couple of miles away, you are unlikely to encounter anyone save a fellow walker or fisherman.

A metal footbridge spans Harwood Dale Beck near its confluence with the River Derwent and our route now angles right, climbing determinedly into Hingles Wood. A path to the right by a bench can be ignored but where the slope levels off you need to keep right, soon walking uphill again to easier ground covered with a deep carpet of pine needles.

Ahead at a track intersection you turn up left, emerging into a forest ride near a marker post. From here a bracken-fringed path—the final metres of ascent—rises to meet a rough forestry road at the summit of Barns Cliff End.

Two hundred metres along to the left there are breathtaking views in clear weather over the Derwent's upper valley and forest-clad moors to the west. Even an hour of hiking in deep woodland—and it will not have taken you much longer than that since leaving Broxa—attunes the senses to close range. Details of pathside vegetation, microcosms of the forest environment, have monopolised your attention so it may be with wide-eyed astonishment that you now survey distant horizons!

The prospect west and south from Barns Cliff End gives you some idea of the extent of Forestry Commission planting in this part of Yorkshire: in fact, 18 per cent of the National Park is afforested, having begun back in 1920 on land

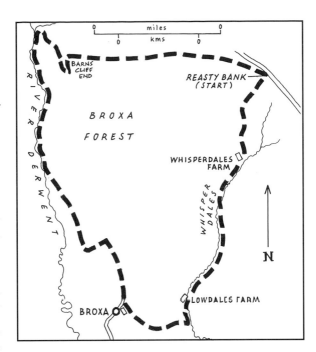

Overleaf: *In Broxa Forest above Lang Dale.*

north of Thornton Dale. Things have expanded dramatically since then of course, but only trees at around the fiftieth year of life are considered mature enough for economical felling. Even so, about 120 acres of Dalby Forest alone are cleared and re-stocked each year, yielding a prodigious 20,000 tons of timber.

The Forestry Commission's role has developed considerably since the early days. Such diverse activities as the management of wildlife habitats and provision of recreational facilities have been added to simple timber production: not all are mutually compatible. On the whole, walkers are welcome on the Commission's land

provided they show consideration for the forest environment by avoiding fire risks and disturbance to wildlife and take litter home.

As it curves round eastwards back towards Reasty Bank car park, the forestry road passes many splendid viewpoints to the north. From this elevated position, the concrete roadways and foundations of Low North Camp are clearly visible, overgrown with gorse as they are since wartime occupation. You can hardly go wrong now and by keeping left at track forks, the broad, pitted road delivers you without complication back to Reasty Bank Top.

WALK 23: *The Hole of Horcum, Malo Cross and the Bridestones*

Terrain: Good hillside, woodland and field paths throughout, with moderate gradients. A steep country road between Lockton and Levisham.
Start/Finish: Levisham. **Distance:** 12 miles (19.5km)—allow 5 to 6 hours. **Maps:** OS Landranger Sheets 94 and 100; Outdoor Leisure South-East sheet.

Reached from the A169 via Lockton and a ferociously steep zig- zag hill, the sleepy village of Levisham sits on the gentle southern slopes of Levisham Moor surrounded by fields. Thirteen hundred years ago, the settlement was described by the ecclesiastical historian Bede as being set among 'steep and solitary hills, where you would rather look for the hiding places of robbers or the lairs of wild animals than the abodes of men'—a comment on the wildness and scarcity of permanent habitation at the time. Indeed, even today deep-sided valleys (locally 'griffs') and the broad trench of Newton Dale tend to isolate Levisham, more especially outside the holiday season when visitors drive down the cul-de-sac lane to the North York Moors Railway station.

Broad greens backed by picturesque cottages and farmhouses flank Levisham's only street, at the top of which will be found a small post office/store and the hospitable Horseshoe Inn. Were it not for the presence of motor cars, the village would be hard to date at first glance, its spaciousness and traditional stone buildings so clearly belonging to earlier times. (Car parking space in the village should be chosen with care so as not to block access or obstruct passing vehicles.)

Few walks in the National Park encompass scenery of such variety as this one, or pass so many absorbing features in the span of a dozen miles. It begins by forking right past the Post Office along the walled Limpsey Gate Lane, a dead-end for motorists. Before long the surface deteriorates and a gentle downhill gradient brings you to the boundary of open moorland. From the gate and stile you cut down to the right over short turf and on through bracken to join the main path down Dundale Griff. The stream bed is usually dry at first, but as you lose height and enter an intimate, densely wooded fold of small hills where Pigtrough, Dundale and Water griffs meet Levisham Beck, running water is at last in evidence. Dundale Beck is crossed on stepping stones and Levisham Beck on a plank footbridge before the path, having swung north, leads on, caught for a while between beck and wall.

As you walk up the valley of Horcum Slack, ridge tops to the left and right are crowned with woodland—even the stream bed itself is tree-choked—and there is a gradual opening out towards the Hole of Horcum. A stile or two later, you are approaching Low Horcum, one of two farms working the land in this great moorland hollow until the late 1960s. High Horcum Farm

to the north has all but disappeared, but Low Horcum, its buildings and gardens for many years abandoned to the elements, has been recently renovated.

Here on its floor, you can enjoy a classic view of the Hole of Horcum—as impressive as any from its rim. Myths and legends surround the Hole, believed in more superstitious times than our own to have been hollowed out by the giant Horcum. A more scientific explanation attributes its formation to undermining by springs and erosion by torrents escaping from an ice-dammed lake which filled Eskdale during the last Ice Age 12,000 years ago; the same water excavated the course of Newton Dale just to the west. This huge natural basin with its steep and accessible enclosing hillsides holds obvious attractions for hang-gliders and model aircraft enthusiasts; it is also traversed by walkers on the long-distance North York Moors Crosses Walk and the Cleveland Way 'Missing Link'.

From Low Horcum, the way continues over grass, dropping to a stile and crossing the infant Levisham Beck. A clear scar of a track mounts the shoulder of hillside ahead and it is towards this that you now climb through bracken. At the top of an eroded groove—escape from the Hole achieved—you reach a stile and a hairpin bend on the busy A169 at Saltergate Bank. Quite unexpectedly, Fylingdales Ballistic Missile Early Warning Station stands close by to the north-east above a rim of moor, while Newton Dale and the great sweep of Levisham Moor monopolise western horizons.

Grassy paths mercifully flank the main road, up which you walk, past a large barn and round towards the roadside car park. Here are more classic views of the Hole of Horcum, its rolling, stream-cut sides falling to the sinuous, elongated tuck of Levisham Beck. You soon turn left onto a public bridleway lane leading to Newgate Foot Farm. This so-called 'Old Wife's Way' was an old packhorse route named, possibly, after an itinerant tinker woman selling knick-knacks to moorland farmers' wives. Immediately beyond a farm gate the way turns left on a stony track between a conifer belt and sheep pasture and in a further 350m you are out on the springy turf of Saltergate Brow. Like other ancient ways across the moors, this escarpment bridleway was once used, as its name implies, to transport salt to the coast and salted fish back inland. Other goods would have included lime for the acid moorland soils and, no doubt, unspecified quantities of smuggled contraband.

Newton Dale gorge is seen well from this elevated situation, as are the heathery expanses of moor to the north, across which the A169 provides a tenuous channel of communication. More likely to command attention, however, are the 'radomes' of RAF Fylingdales from which the famous '4-minute warning' of nuclear attack would emanate. Radar installations inside the 160ft (49m) high fibreglass 'golf balls' monitor 3000 miles (4828km) of air space from Turkey to the Arctic and are complemented by similar stations at Clear in Alaska and at Thule in Greenland.

Previous page: **At Low Bridestones.**

Keeping to the bank edge, the old grassy track crosses twin furrows at Double Dike, a Bronze Age earthwork connecting the head of Long Gill with Saltergate Brow, then swings east. Soon you begin to descend gently through bracken, furze and scrub towards the hard dark edge of Allerston Forest on Blakey Rigg. Inscribed with initials and pitted from centuries of erosion, Malo Cross stands below Whinny Nab where the way veers south—an ancient, evocative landmark on the salt route to Whitby.

Following a well walked path which diverges from the forest edge, you reach a gate and contour over broad pastureland below Hazlehead Moor, with dramatic views of Blakey Topping to the east. Rising on a beeline for Newgate Foot farmhouse and negotiating a couple of stiles, you reach a concrete access lane. Given the necessary time and inclination, an ascent of Blakey Topping can be easily made by turning left down the lane and in 400m, at a track crossroads, climbing through bracken direct to the heathery summit. As well as signs of an ancient stone circle, views are tremendous, especially over the western section of Dalby Forest which lies on the land like a deep-pile rug.

At the lane top on Newgate Brow, a left turn is taken near a National Trust 'Bridestones' sign, where a gate gives onto Grime Moor. Level walking, past fields and far-reaching views, aims

for forest but skirts it to the right at the last moment. Thereafter, good firm going over low heather leads on to the marshy top of Bridestones Griff and a right turn towards the Bridestones themselves. Many such-named rocks occur on the North York Moors and are almost certainly associated with ancient fertility rites, though some believe the name derives from the Norse for 'edge' or 'brink'. First to be encountered on the south side of Bridestones Griff are the Low Bridestones, a group of weathered, pinkish-grey sandstone rocks, one of which bulges top-heavy on a narrowing stem. Wind, rain and frost continue imperceptibly to modify the surface and shapes of these sentinels of hard, siliceous sandstone—a process that has been going on for some 60,000 years. By retracing steps for 200m and turning down left over Bridestones Griff, you can explore the High Bridestones whose arches, cavities and eroded ledges are no less compelling. In a landscape of long, rolling horizons, these outcrops have the impact of punctuation marks; they are astonishing features, sculptural, tactile—living geology!

The public enjoys concessionary access to Bridestones Moor and Dove Dale woods, administered jointly by the National Trust and the Yorkshire Naturalists' Trust, but we are asked not to stray from paths or damage plants and trees. Well known spots such as this exist on a

knife-edge between on the one hand satisfying public curiosity—the sightseeing element—and on the other becoming damaged by human erosion and careless behaviour. Fortunately the Bridestones can only be reached on foot, either from the Dalby Forest toll road at Stain Dale or by the walk being described. Nevertheless, the potential threat from increasing numbers of visitors cannot be ignored.

Heading south now along Needle Point—a narrowing, heather-clad ridge between Dovedale and Bridestones griffs—you descend steeply, cross a stream and walk through the beautiful mixed woodland of Dove Dale. Birch and Scots Pine here are indigenous, unlike the Forestry Commission's vast plantings of foreign conifer species. After turning left to recross the stream and pass through a squeeze-stile, you veer sharp right, back over the stream and onto a track to Low Staindale.

About half a mile (1km) to the east along a clear path lies Staindale Water, created in recent years to attract more varied wildlife. Picnic areas, car park and toilets have been provided and form part of Dalby Forest Drive, a toll road

meandering scenically from just north of Thornton Dale village to Langdale End near Hackness in the Derwent Valley. Low Dalby, a forestry village created in 1949, now houses a Visitor Centre selling books, maps and souvenirs, including leaflets on short, waymarked forest trails. In addition to a fascinating exhibition of the Forestry Commission's work and an imaginative audio-visual wildlife display, Low Dalby provides refreshments and generous parking, making it an ideal base for a day's exploration of the adjacent forest.

Below the buildings of Low Staindale, you cross a double stile and follow a track through pasture alongside Staindale Beck. Beyond a small pumping station, a stile leads into Holm Woods; Dalby Forest Drive, which has shadowed us on the other side of the beck right down Stain Dale, soon swings away south, but the walk continues ahead over pasture by a large oak tree to a huddle of barns. Two gates later you pass round the front of Staindale Lodge and into the mixed trees of Hagg Wood. Its early origins now fully manifest, the 'hollow way'—a track worn to a sunken groove—takes you up through the most delightful woodland above Rustifhead Slack. Open fields, electricity pylons and the A169 return you to civilisation and straight ahead lies Lockton village, with its church, shops, pub and youth hostel. Main road traffic is soon out of sight and out of mind!

Towards the village's far end, you keep right, down Mill Bank Road and past a splendid viewpoint over the wooded confluence of Wedland Slack and Levisham Beck at St Robert's Well—dramatic stream valleys dissecting an upland plateau. Levisham seems no distance away as the crow flies, but a substantial 'down and up' on the country road is involved to reach journey's end. At the valley bottom you pass the old mill, once the centre of a thriving little community, and must then gird up your loins for a brutally steep climb round a 1 in 3 hairpin—a sting in the tail if ever there was one!

Above: **Weather-sculpted siliceous sandstone — Low Bridestones.**

Left: **The old bridleway on Saltergate Brow.**

Facing page: **Emerging from the wooded confines of Horcum Slack.**

WALK 24: *Levisham Moor and the Hole of Horcum*

Terrain: Clear moorland and field paths with a final steep climb. **Start/Finish:** The roadside car park on Saltergate Bank, 2½ miles (4km) north of Lockton on the A169 Pickering to Whitby road. **Distance:** 5 miles (8km)—allow about 3 hours. **Maps:** OS Landranger Sheets 94 and 100; Outdoor Leisure South-East sheet.

The Hole of Horcum is such an extraordinary feature that a walk exploring both its moorland rim and its pastoral floor is well worth taking. It is not a long outing and the way is easy, yet it encompasses a wealth of interest and scenic variety.

Motorists use the Saltergate Bank car park—mid-way along the moor road between Pickering and Whitby—as a convenient stopping point and during the summer months there is usually a refreshment van parked there. For walkers it represents a good, high-level start for routes to the east and west taking in Newton Dale, Levisham and Lockton villages, Blakey Topping, The Bridestones and the western section of Dalby Forest.

Immediately you cross the road—which can be busy—and walk north along the rough grassy bank above Horcum Wood, you are savouring classic views of the Hole of Horcum. From this angle, Levisham Beck snakes down the valley floor, its course draining the folds of hillside above. This entire natural amphitheatre, three-quarters of a mile (1.2km) wide, was formed some

Levisham Moor (distant right) and the Hole of Horcum.

12,000 years ago during the last Ice Age. Torrents of meltwater escaping from an ice-dammed lake which filled Esk Dale—an east-west valley to the north virtually linking the Cleveland Plain with Whitby—excavated many of the land forms we know today on its headlong surge towards lower ground and the sea. Intensive undermining by springs is also thought to have contributed to the Hole of Horcum's formation: certainly it appears as a sunken basin rather than a conventional valley such as Newton Dale just to the west. A more colourful explanation indicts the Giant Horcum who, so the legend goes, scooped up a handful of earth to throw at his wife! He missed, incidentally, and the gargantuan clod formed Blakey Topping, 2 miles (3.2km) to the east!

By shadowing the main road, you soon swing west where it plunges in a steep hairpin towards Saltergate Inn at the bottom of the bank.

Right off the road bend, a stile and gate lead ahead onto a good stony track; if you find yourself descending either left or right, you have missed the correct way.

At first you hug the curving edge of the Hole but in half a mile the track trends away from it along the upper slopes of Levisham Moor. Beyond the top of Horness Griff ('griff' is colloquial for side valley), a gentle descent brings you to Seavy Pond, a watery declivity on heather moor top at the head of Hawdale Griff. The Hole itself has become obscured from view by intervening Broadhead, Sheephouse and Horness riggs, with 'griffs' now the more prominent landmark.

Levisham Moor is scattered with prehistoric earthworks and enclosures. One such—Cross Dyke, stretching west towards West Side Brow above Newton Dale—was probably a territorial boundary constructed by Iron Age settlers some 2000 years ago. It is a conspicuous enough feature even today, though the earthworks associated with a fortified farmstead of similar date are hard to identify.

A mile further south the unequivocal path leads you to Dundale Pond. As an information plate tells us, the small valley was given to the monks of Malton Priory in about 1230 as pasture for their cattle, sheep and horses. It is likely that the pond was dug at about this time as a watering hole for stock. An interesting relic of this old land-use is that a few local people still own common grazing rights on Levisham Moor.

This is the turning point of the walk in two senses: open moorland is left behind for wooded valleys and the return leg is started by taking the path left down Dundale Griff. Picturesque Levisham with its welcoming pub the Horseshoe Inn lies less than a mile straight on along Limpsey Gate Lane, an easy extension to the route. To the right, a path leads down to Levisham Sta-

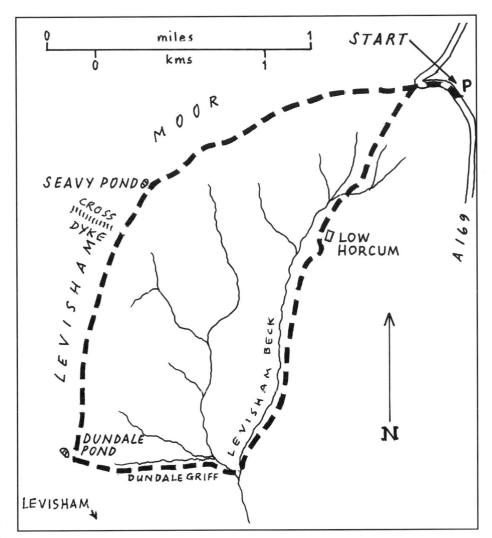

tion on the North York Moors steam railway, another possible detour.

Partly hidden by trees, the bed of Dundale Griff is usually dry but does show signs of life following heavy rain. The way drops intimately into a tree-choked fold of small hills at the conjunction of Pigtrough, Dundale and Water griffs; contrasts with Levisham Moor's exposed top could hardly be more strongly drawn, especially in windy weather. At a sign you turn left to cross Dundale Beck on stepping stones and Levisham Beck by plank footbridge. Caught between beck and wall along the foot of Far Black Rigg, the path heads towards an anticipated opening out of enclosing hillsides. As you leave the wooded confines of Horcum Slack and cross a stile onto grassy slopes, keeping up right to join a higher path line, exciting views beckon.

Soon the buildings of Low Horcum are approached and the great scalloped, hollowed flanks of the Hole appear to their best advantage. Until the 1960s, two farms worked the valley land here. Low Horcum, surrounded by

thistles and the abject remains of a domestic garden at my first visit has, happily, been renovated. Of High Horcum, once situated under the northern rim of the hollow, nothing has survived.

You keep left of Low Horcum and walk ahead over grass, dropping across a feeder stream of Levisham Beck and climbing gently through bracken. There can be no mistaking the path: several long-distance walking routes incorporate it, including the Cleveland Way's 'Missing Link' and the North York Moors Crosses Walk. By now your exit from the Hole will be perfectly obvious—a scar of a track running up the valley perimeter's shoulder. In fact, the passage of countless feet and the draining of storm water have etched a deeply eroded groove up which you must climb for about 200ft (60m) to a stile at the A169 hairpin. Views during the 300m back to the car park span most of the ground covered—always a satisfying finale to an enjoyable hike.

WALK 25: *Levisham, Newton Dale and the North York Moors Railway*

Terrain: A steep descent, then woodland tracks, hillside and field paths— muddy in places. **Start/Finish:** Levisham. **Distance:** $5\frac{1}{4}$ miles (8.5km)— allow about 3 hours. **Maps:** OS Landranger Sheets 94 and 100; Outdoor Leisure South-East sheet.

Although it crosses some fine country, this walk will, I suspect, revolve for most people around the North York Moors Railway—at least during the spring, summer and autumn when trains are running. Thousands of holidaymakers each year are attracted to the steam-hauled journey between Pickering and Grosmont, a nostalgic journey for lovers of steam trains and a highly scenic one through the moorsides and forests of Newton Dale.

Many hikers enjoy combining train travel with walks of great quality by alighting at Levisham, Newtondale or Goathland in the morning and catching a return service to Pickering or Grosmont later in the day. Throughout the main holiday season, trains run hourly. You do not need to be a passenger to experience the thrill of steam locomotives—this walk, for one, will provide you with distant and close-up views of trains, both in motion and waiting at Levisham station.

Like Walk 23, we start at Levisham village. There can be few more pleasant places to begin or end a walk than the Horseshoe Inn, situated at the top of the main street. Here, if the weather is smiling, you can sit outside with a meal or a drink and contemplate the delights of this sleepy community. Spacious grassy verges backed by farm buildings and cottages, and the absence of significant through traffic, make for greater peace than one would expect in such a pretty spot. A complete sense of timelessness is betrayed only by the presence of motor-cars and carefully renovated façades.

Levisham stands at around 560ft (170m) on a plateau between Newton Dale to the west and a cluster of 'griffs' (side valleys) to the east. Its elevation will not escape your notice, for this walk, starting from the south end of the village, dives into undergrowth at a sign on the left, short-cutting a viciously steep road hairpin. Below the main bend, you take a bridleway to the right (not the track at the apex of the road bend itself) and in 150m branch left onto a grassy track past St Mary's Church.

A steady decline in the number of church-goers combined with the amalgamation of parishes and the dispersal of rural communities has sounded the death knell for more than one country church in a remote situation. St Mary's, alas, is one such victim of changing times. Its origins date back to the period of the Norman Conquest and it is said to contain interesting carvings of even greater antiquity.

Facing page: ***A train leaving Levisham station.***

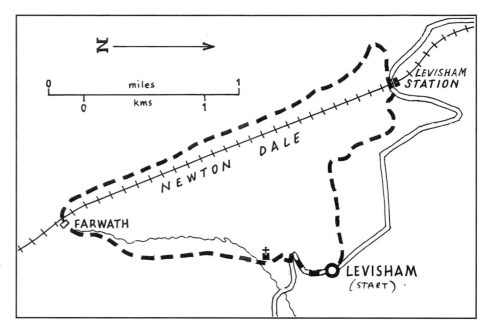

Crossing Levisham Beck by footbridge, you walk along its banks and up a track, in 100m turning right onto the Sleights Road track which takes you gently, if muddily, downhill between picturesque old hawthorn trees. Entering woods, you contour along above the beck and emerge into open pastureland, turning right through a gate. Close now to the beck and the wooded spur opposite of Ness Head, a good track leads you to the buildings of Farwath by the railway line in Newton Dale—a fine location for train-spotting!

This hamlet in the back-of-beyond was home to a thriving cottage industry making 'besoms' (heather brooms) around the turn of the last century. You can still find besoms here and there in local shops but they were once used extensively in the shipyards and to skim slag off molten metal.

Railway and watercourse—virtually at the confluence of Levisham and Pickering becks—are crossed by footbridge, whereafter a broad track on the right and a subsequent right fork will set you on Bottoms Road. There is an aptness to the name as underfoot conditions become unpromisingly squelchy in the region of Chalybente Spring! However, beyond a conifer plantation the going rapidly improves. Glimpses of the railway along here are tantalisingly few—frustrating in the extreme should a train pass and all you see is smoke!

Our track narrows to a rather overgrown path negotiating several gates and climbing easily across rough pasture. Two fields later it deteriorates again, spoiled by intrusions of bracken and scrub through East Brow Wood, especially in high summer. Further ascent is rewarded by a clearer trod in open country, parallel at first to an overhead power line then passing beneath it. Half-way across the next well-grazed field you veer sharp right down a shallow, gorse-filled depression to meet another clear footpath, not far from the village of Newton-on-Rawcliffe.

Views of Newton Dale are, at last, comprehensive, its glacial origins apparent. During a late stage of the last Ice Age some 12,000 years ago, vast quantities of water overflowing from the lake which filled Eskdale to the north were prevented from escaping to the sea by ice moving down the coast. Instead, the meltwater roared south, scouring out the deep, snaking course of Newton Dale gorge from the head of the Murk Esk valley to the Vale of Pickering.

Even before George Stephenson had pioneered a railway through Newton Dale from Pickering to Whitby in the 1830s, plans had been mooted for a canal to link inland markets with the coast. Such an undertaking would have been immense, however, and the idea of a railway route was always more realistic.

Initially, horses pulled a single coach along the rails but after George Hudson purchased and improved the track in the late 1840s, steam locomotives were introduced. The line's operating life as part of Britain's national rail network lasted a mere two decades, ended, as so many rural services were, by Dr Beeching's axe in 1964.

There is no quelling the legendary enthusiasm of railway buffs whose hard work finally led to the line's successful re-opening. Operated by the independent North York Moors Historical Railway Trust, trains run from Easter to the end of October and at Christmas, with the highest frequency in June, July and August. Services connect at Grosmont with British Rail's Esk Valley

line to Whitby.

Descending a clear track through trees and crossing a footbridge, you meet the road near Levisham station. Everything from fire buckets to ticket office, from flowers to platform waiting room belong to a past era of railway history. The arrival of a steam train is sure to bring a lump to the throats of those with childhood memories of sufficient vintage.

You take your leave along the country road towards Levisham but in 100m turn right past a cattle grid onto a public footpath. Once over a stream and through a gate, it climbs through quite exquisite woodland and up a field edge towards corrugated-iron sheds at Grove House. Here you bear right to a stile and walk up a pleasant grassy path angling diagonally across steep hillside at a gentle gradient. There are marvellous valley views above drifts of foxgloves.

The path levels off at another superlative viewpoint by a wooden bench where you ignore a hollow way off to the left, instead contouring rather excitingly on a narrow trod round the head of Keldgate Slack. A final few metres of ascent past gorse bushes and ever wider panoramas to the west bring you to a gate-stile and a left turn along fields on the plateau. The way joins Little Field Lane, turns a last corner and confronts you with the welcome prospect of the Horseshoe Inn.

Above: **The intriguing detail of steam locomotives.**

Top left: **Beside Levisham's village street.**

Bottom left: **Levisham station.**

Facing page: **Springtime in the Forge Valley Nature Reserve.**

WALK 26: *Hackness, The River Derwent and Forge Valley*

Terrain: Undulating field paths, a little road walking, then level riverside and woodland paths. Can be muddy after rain. **Start/Finish:** West Ayton. **Distance:** 10 miles (16km)—allow 5 to 6 hours.**Maps:** OS Landranger Sheet 101; Outdoor Leisure South-East sheet.

This walk almost forms a figure of eight. Where the outward and return legs approach within a few hundred metres of each other (near the Forge Valley picnic site), you could quite easily split the route into separate loops. However, taken in its entirety, there are few hikes in the National Park that offer such variety of scenery and features of interest along the way.

West and East Ayton straddle the River Derwent on the busy A170 Thirsk to Scarborough road which runs along the southern perimeter of the Park. You may notice an imposing ruined tower on high ground above West Ayton, but more of that later when we pass close by. You start by crossing the Derwent, passing the Forge Valley/Hackness road and, just beyond East Ayton's church (much of it thirteenth century and worth a look round), turning left into Moor Road. This will take you up past a housing estate into open country right on the National Park boundary.

At a 'Road Narrows' sign, you fork left on a good track through woods. A couple of field widths away to the left are disused and partly overgrown quarries from which oolite—a fine-grained, warm coloured limestone—was extracted. Emerging from the trees, you veer left a little then walk ahead, due north, on a grassy track along by a hedge.

Although marked as a definitive right of way on Ordnance Survey maps, the start had been ploughed up at my last visit and it is to be hoped that the rest of it escapes the same fate. By obliterating paths, farmers do not, of course, remove our right to walk across their land—providing we do so on the correct line and avoid damaging crops—but I always feel it suggests thinly veiled indifference to the interests of the walking fraternity.

Gaining height very gradually, you reach the small tree belt of Whin Covert and turn left past Skell Dikes. The adjacent plateau is dotted with tumuli and earthworks—though most have succumbed to the plough—and Skell Dikes, its walls overgrown with hawthorn, was almost certainly a prehistoric land boundary.

The unmetalled farm lane will lead you past views over the Vale of Pickering to Osborne Lodge Farm, a distinctive complex of traditional farm buildings refreshingly unspoiled by modern development. Through the farmyard, you take a gate on the right out into a field above Ruston Cliff Wood. Half way along, another gate in the farm's boundary wall provides access to a narrow path downhill through woodland; steeper for a while, it levels off and deposits you by the Forge Valley road at Green Gate.

Forge Valley Picnic Area and viewpoint lies to the left. Should you wish to make a short-cut return to West Ayton, simply walk back down the road for about 500m where, from a

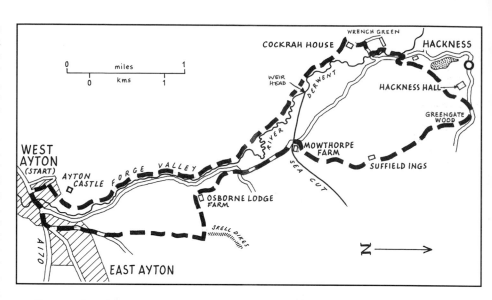

small car park, a footbridge crosses the River Derwent. Turn left along its west bank through the delightful Forge Valley woods—details appear towards the end of this walk's description.

You now drop down Mowthorp Road past neat bungalows to Mowthorp Bridge, spanning Sea Cut. Interestingly, this was the River Derwent's original course, but towards the end of the last Ice Age the still-frozen North Sea forced meltwater from the land through a narrow valley to the south. With the final melting of the ice, immense quantities of water were released, scouring the Forge Valley gorge we know today and rendering the Vale of Pickering permanently susceptible to flooding. To alleviate the problem and improve the Vale's farmland, Sea Cut was excavated in the mid-1800's, diverting excess water from the Derwent east to the sea at Scalby, near Scarborough.

Water-flow into the Derwent and Sea Cut respectively is controlled at Weir Head; a careful balance is required to satisfy the needs of wildlife and vegetation in Forge Valley and even, I am told, to keep local anglers happy!

If you walk into Mowthorp Farm's entrance, straight ahead between barns and through a gate, you will find yourself climbing a grassy, sunken track flanked by hawthorn trees. From a white gate at the top, the right of way continues for 100m alongside Holly Wood before veering left uphill across a field to a gate in the lower edge of Hawthorn Wood. However, if crops are growing it is probably best to walk straight on up the field edge, keeping in single file if in a group.

A continuation of the hollow way leads up through Hawthorn Wood, secretive and overgrown, to a field corner gate. A turn half-left here along by a hedge takes you to Sutton Ings Farm, which is passed to the right, and onto a broad, stony field track. Beyond the metalled

Limestone Lane and the entrance to Suffield Heights, you cross a stile onto a semi-surfaced track. About 15m before it swings right to a disused quarry at a 'Private—Keep Out' sign, you must watch carefully for a rather indistinct path (at the time of writing) which dives down left by a fence post into a bushy hollow.

Like so many footpaths in this and other regions of Britain, it has suffered from under-use, a curious obverse of the more publicised problems of over-use. It seems as if footpaths need walkers in modest numbers to maintain a kind of equilibrium: too few and they become obscured by vegetation or lose their viability to obstructions or even the plough; too many and we encounter the serious erosion typified by parts of the Pennine Way or Lake District fell routes.

Our onward way descends into trees past an impressive old lime kiln. Undergrowth soon thins and beyond a handgate a small dry valley heads down through Greengate Wood. You cross a stile at the bottom and angle down left to the road about 750m east of Hackness village.

If time allows, a short detour past the entrance to Hackness Hall is worthwhile. St Hilda of Whitby Abbey established a nunnery here in 680, but even this out-of-the-way retreat did not prove immune to the attentions of invading Danes who destroyed it in 867. Two hundred years later the nunnery was rebuilt, enjoying a new lease of life until the Dissolution of the Monasteries in 1539. An inscribed Saxon cross in the church, and the village lake in which fish would have been bred for food, are, sadly, the house's only remaining relics.

Hackness, with its picturesque village school and post office, stands at the head of several dales, spread finger-like to the north and west. Its relative popularity is heightened by its proximity to the Dalby Forest drive at Langdale End

and to Scarborough.

At a footpath sign 250m or so east of Hackness Hall, you walk up away from the road onto an old track following a shallow ledge just below Greengate Wood. Climbing gently round to the left, it rises to a stile and continues over pasture towards a line of trees. From this elevation there are excellent views over Hackness Hall, views denied to motorists by a screen of trees. Presently belonging to Lord Derwent, this stately Georgian manor was designed by the York architect John Carr and was once the home of the first woman diarist, Lady Hoby.

Staying outside the woods above Hackness lake and crossing a double wire fence, the path contours over rough grazing land, eventually dropping in a zig-zag to a stile at the road beyond Mill farm. Opposite, the River Derwent is crossed by footbridge, whereafter you turn left along the raised river bank fringed with gorse.

The remainder of the walk follows the Derwent's course so gradients are negligible, though the slopes of West Ayton and Coverdale moors rise immediately to the west, topped by mixed woodland. At the road bridge near Wrench Green you turn right to reach Rose Cottage at a T-junction by a cul-de-sac sign and walk past Cockrah House barns to a waymarked gate. Aiming left towards the bottom of hillocky pasture, you begin to accompany the river closely through fields until the footbridges of Weir Head are in view.

Although not directly beside the path, the weir is no more than 100m away and is worth a look. Heading east through flat fields, the big Sea Cut drain funnels off a good proportion of the Derwent's water: hereafter, the river seems noticeably depleted, a mere shadow of its former self.

Waymarked stiles and gates define the way forward over rough water meadow

occasionally close to the river but often remote from its sinuous meanders. About 1 km beyond Sea Cut weir, the Derwent swings away in a large loop to the east, but the walk continues straight on, past a marshy area of springs on the right, towards the wooded corner of Spikers Hill ahead.

When the river is rejoined at a stile, you enter the Forge Valley Nature Reserve, a magnificent culmination to this varied hike. The woodland here is an authentic remnant of the forest which covered much of Britain in prehistoric times and retains many original characteristics—oaks on higher, well drained ground, mixed elm and ash on the flushed slopes, with willow and alder in the moist valley bottom. Bird life is widely represented, including such species as wood and willow warblers, nuthatches, woodpeckers, chaffinches and chiffchaffs.

Enclaves of natural woodland such as this have survived despite man's relentless encroachment. Land clearance, the grazing of animals and the use of timber for building and burning (notably here in forges, after which the valley is named) have all contributed to the demise of old moorland forests.

Duckboarding has been laid over long stretches of riverside path to protect the banks from erosion—a wise and necessary measure, for many people visit this delectable wooded valley, bird watchers, naturalists, anglers and walkers among them. Two footbridges about 500m apart provide access to small car parks and bird feeding stations off the valley road opposite, but otherwise there are no interruptions in $1\frac{1}{2}$ miles (2.5km) of pure, unalloyed delight!

Ultimately you leave the Nature Reserve itself and pass a weir; where the strip of land ahead narrows between the river and Stonyflat Wood, you keep to the field edge alongside trees to reach a gate. The ensuing stony track takes you close to the 20ft (6m) high ruins of a fourteenth-century fortified tower belonging to Ayton Castle. Between the twelfth and fifteenth centuries it was the stronghold of the Eures family, a descendant of which, Sir Ralph Eures, would become governor of Scarborough Castle in the early 1500's. Though not a castle in the strict sense, the ruin, set on elevated ground, exudes a kind of faded, mellowed echo of its noble origins.

Ayton Castle is effectively the walk's full stop. To reach the starting point, go through a kissing gate to a minor road by houses, where a left turn will take you downhill to the A170 at West Ayton.

Top: **Hackness Hall from the path below Greengate Wood.**

Bottom: **The evocative ruin of Ayton Castle marks the walk's conclusion.**

Facing page: **The bold profile of Ana Cross on Spaunton Moor.**

WALK 27: *Rydale Folk Museum and Spaunton Moor*

Terrain: Field paths, a little country road walking and good tracks over rough heather moorland. **Start/Finish:** Hutton-le-Hole. **Distance:** 8½ miles (14km)—allow 4 hours actual walking time. **Maps:** OS Landranger Sheet 100; Outdoor Leisure South-West sheet.

Starting and finishing a walk at a village as attractive and hospitable as Hutton-le-Hole is pleasure enough, whatever the weather. Add a visit to the fascinating Ryedale Folk Museum and an exhilarating tramp over wild but gently angled heather moorland and you have all the ingredients for a grand day out.

Finds of pottery, arrowheads and other artifacts around Hutton-le-Hole pre-date recorded history, pointing to a succession of early settlement by man, from Neolithic farmers and herdsmen, through the Bronze Age to the Roman and Saxon eras. Registered in the great Domesday survey of 1085-6 as Hoton, the village subsequently underwent several name changes, including Hege-Hoton, Hoton under Heg, Hewton, Hutton-in-the-Hole and, by the nineteenth century, Hutton-le-Hole.

As its name implies, the settlement lies in a hollow between two limestone headlands of the flat-topped Tabular Hills which slope gently south, forming a marked contrast to the open moors further north. One's impressions are of an immensely picturesque village green, non-

Below: **Spaunton Lodge (distant left) and Hutton Ridge (skyline) from Blakey Ridge.**

chalantly grazed by sheep and surrounded by a haphazard scattering of charming cottages. Several bridges span Hutton and Fairy Call becks as they tumble in little waterfalls through a picture-postcard scene which draws thousands of visitors every year.

Perhaps English country villages appeal to our collective yearning to escape the complex, pressing issues of our time into a life of Arcadian simplicity. They are reassuring, manageable places, the more so for their tea rooms, antique shops, friendly pubs and somewhere for the coaches to park!

Hutton-le-Hole has fostered a long tradition of crafts through the centuries. Spinning and weaving, tanning and milling, lime burning, coal and ironstone mining have all left their mark on the area—earthy origins superseded today by manicured lawns and self-conscious prettiness.

The realities of our ancestors' bucolic existence would not match our fantasies. Life was hard without what now pass for the 'basic necessities',—electricity, labour-saving devices and assured supplies of food—but a true appreciation of the differences is difficult to invoke without tangible clues. Books will stimulate the imagination, but nothing gets us quite so close to the past as seeing and touching the tools, implements and buildings used in daily life many years ago. The Ryedale Folk Museum helps make that link with the past and is well worth an hour or two's browse before or after the walk. Opened in 1964, it contains the private collection of the Crosland family and is housed in $2\frac{1}{2}$ acres bequeathed specifically for the purpose. Virtually all the material has been collected from the locality and reflects Ryedale life two or three centuries ago. There is no space here for the detail, but exhibits include entire reconstructed buildings, shops and workshops, farm machinery, country craft implements, a stable, glass furnace, foundries, barns and many archaeological remains.

Just south of the museum (which doubles as an Information Centre), a path leaves from behind the chapel, keeping left of the bowling green and crossing a series of fields. Fairy Call Beck—an arm of Loskey Beck which rises $2\frac{1}{2}$ miles (4km) to the north and which will be encountered later—is crossed by footbridge, whereafter you rise to join the country road towards Lastingham. Just before it swings right

Above: **Hutton Beck, Hutton-le-Hole.**

Below: **Old ironstone kilns at Rosedale Bank Top.**

over Loskey Beck, you turn off left on a grassy track beside allotments and hawthorn hedges; beyond a gate, the broad track narrows to path width outside the moorland intake wall. Past Camomile Farm and a steep little down-and-up to cross Hole Beck, you arrive at the moor gate a few hundred metres above Lastingham.

In many ways Lastingham's old houses, grouped together along two streets, have more to commend them architecturally than those at Hutton-le-Hole, though fewer visitors by far come here during the tourist season. A cluster of shops and one or two refreshment places complete the village amenities, but before taking your leave do call at the church. It contains a superbly preserved Norman crypt dating from around 1080 when monks from Whitby Abbey re-established a monastery here on the ruins of an earlier Benedictine Abbey destroyed by the Danes in 862.

To resume the walk, steps are retraced up a cul-de-sac lane to the large tree and moor gate north of the village. Ahead stretches a swelling moorland horizon and by trending left of the initial hollow you will pick up a good grassy track climbing gently along the broad shoulder of Lastingham Ridge. To the east lie Spring Heads and the valley of Tranmire Beck, but Hole Beck, to the west, is hidden for a while by higher ground.

A succession of cairns marks the way, now sandy underfoot, across the heathery expanses of Spaunton Moor. There can be no mistaking the clear track for the next mile or so, but where it curves north-west at a double cairn you fork left on a narrower path, aiming for the moorland cross visible ahead. Within a few hundred metres, an even less defined trod branches left through the heather but quickly becomes plainer as it approaches Ana Cross.

Fifty or so such structures can be found on the North York Moors, many reduced by the vagaries of erosion and vandalism to socket stones with broken shafts. Ana Cross, however, named after some long-forgotten person whose story will never be known with certainty, remains robust and defiantly intact. Crosses, it is thought, were erected by monasteries to act as navigational beacons and to provide spiritual reassurance for travellers on uninhabited and often intimidating moortops. Even though a lack of hard evidence leaves them surrounded by mystery and enigma, many are named on current OS maps and continue, in a more secular vein perhaps, to guide travellers on foot across these featureless uplands.

Beyond toy-like traffic on the moor road between Hutton-le-Hole and Rosedale, the north-west horizon is interrupted by an antiquity of even earlier date: Three Howes tumuli is one Bronze Age burial site among hundreds

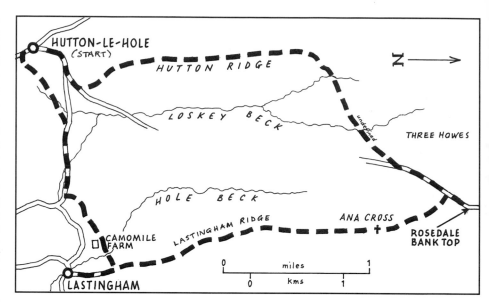

in the region. Leaving Ana Cross, you join a wide track north-west to the road at Rosedale Bank Top. It was here, on March 27th 1861, that the Rosedale Ironstone Railway was officially opened. Ore had been worked on a small scale since Roman times, but a burgeoning demand for iron from heavy industries following the Industrial Revolution led to intensive, if short-lived, extraction on the dalesides. (For more comprehensive details of the ironstone mining operations, see Walk 28.)

The ironstone railway, built to transport ore from Rosedale 14 miles (22.5km) across the moors to Ingleby Incline and thence to the blast furnaces of Teesside, was as an extraordinary undertaking by any yardstick. Its southern terminus here at Bank Top, 975ft (297m) above sea level, sustained a small community of railway employees and their families. All but a couple of their cottages have been demolished, though between 1933 and 1950 one was used as a youth hostel.

Across the road, behind overgrown spoil heaps and hollows, stands the crumbling masonry of eight kilns. In them, ore from Hollins Mines to the south-east was tipped and roasted to drive off water and carbonic acid gas—a process known as calcination—thus reducing the ironstone's weight for transportation. Until 1972 when it was, sad to say, demolished, the Hollins Mines engine-house chimney formed a famous local landmark. Water for the steam boilers driving the winding gear and for railway locos was drawn from a reservoir near Three Howes (still discernible), fed in turn by a leat from an area of marshy lakes called Jewel Mere a mile to the west.

The original roadway climbing to Bank Top was constructed by the ironstone company; at an average gradient of 1 in 3, it is one of

Britain's steepest road hills and was used for hill climbs during the early days of motor sport. From the top there is a fine panorama over Rosedale's tree-patched field patterns and flanking hillsides.

To begin the walk's return leg, the road south-west towards Hutton-le-Hole is followed for half a mile (less than 1km). Beyond grouse butts and a slight left bend, two parallel tracks branch off right, the second of which, grassy at first but soon petering out, establishes your direction over rough heather towards a clear track ahead. The way drops soggily over Loskey Beck to a sheepfold and turns onto the track following a line of shooting butts on Loskey Ridge before descending to ford another arm of Loskey Beck.

Climbing a little, you soon reach an intersection at which walkers are signposted left between two grouse butts on a clear path dropping pleasantly down Hutton Ridge. Views ahead of the Tabular Hills form a delightful counterpoint to the rolling waves of heather and ling surrounding you on three sides, but equally compelling will be the long, richly textured fingers of Blakey Ridge to the west and Spaunton Moor to the east. Eventually you join Lodge Road, a broad, stony access way from Spaunton Lodge. Lower down it is metalled and leads out to the public road just a short distance from the car park at Hutton-le-Hole.

Facing page:

*Top: **Cruck Cottage.***

*Bottom: **The Ryedale Folk Museum.***

Old kilns and ventilation chimney at Low Baring, East Mines.

WALK 28: *The Rosedale Ironstone Railway*

Terrain: Some field paths, but mostly old railway trackbed, rough in places. **Start/Finish:** Thorgill hamlet, at the end of Daleside Road near Rosedale Abbey. **Distance:** 8½ miles (14km)—allow 4 to 5 hours. **Maps:** OS Landranger Sheets 100 and 94; Outdoor Leisure South-West and North-West sheets.

For many generations, inhabitants of Rosedale Abbey and its environs noticed that during thunderstorms lightning often struck a cliff on the dale side near Hollins Farm. No obvious explanation being forthcoming, myths developed of treasure or even the devil himself being buried in the hillside.

In fact, the outcrop was pure ironstone, a deposit of exceptional thickness and highly magnetic. Rock had already been quarried here for roadstone before its true value was recognised, but in 1856 extraction of iron-ore began.

There is good evidence that an iron-works existed in Rosedale in medieval times, but it is thought that the depletion of oak woodland from which furnace charcoal was made, along with transportation difficulties in and out of such a remote valley, led to its eventual closure.

By 1800 ironstone was being collected from shoreline deposits at Saltburn and Scarborough by the Tyne Iron Company—modest operations taking advantage of naturally exposed rock. Mining *per se* was not begun until 1836 when a seam was located running from Grosmont to the coast at Skinningrove; subsequently, other ore fields were found around Guisborough and along the northern scarp of the Cleveland Hills.

These tentative stabs at ironstone exploitation did not in themselves herald the revolution waiting just around the corner. Only with the opening of West Mines—that magnetic cliff above Hollins Farm—and the discovery of further rich veins at Sheriff's Pit to the west of Rosedale Abbey and at East Mines on the dale's opposite flanks, did activity mushroom.

Rosedale was transformed from a rural backwater into the centre of a boom industry. Coal mines were sunk to supply railway engines and steam driven winches, while out on the moors and dale sides there sprung up an infrastructure of railway tracks, sidings, kilns, hoppers, chimneys and rows of dwellings.

Initially, ore had been carted out in horse-drawn wagons to Pickering and thence by rail to various iron-works. But the roadway was atrocious, described at the time as a 'complete bog from end to end, full of clay holes 2 ft deep'. By the early 1870s when extraction had reached its height, a single track, standard gauge line was in use between Battersby, on the main line near Great Ayton, and West Rosedale Bank Top, a distance of 14 miles (22.5km). Wagons were hauled up Ingleby Incline to moortop level by

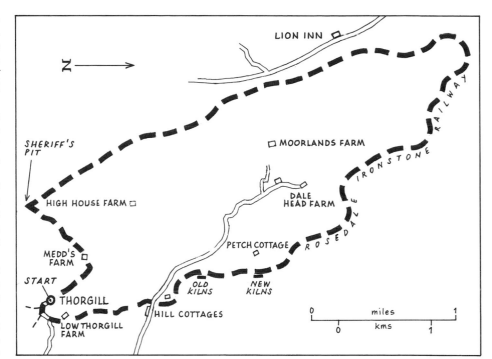

Right: **The remains of Black Houses, East Rosedale.**

steel ropes. In 1865 a spur was added round Rosedale Head to the East Mines complex and it is that trackbed that forms the nucleus of this walk.

A lengthy preamble has been necessary to set the scene, for the walk, more than any in this book, takes us a century back in time and knowing what to look for will heighten your appreciation of a fascinating chapter in Rosedale's history. For the record, it did not last long. After 1920, higher-quality imported ore combined with the effects of the General Strike in 1926 sounded the industry's death knell. With 65 years of operation behind it, the Rosedale Ironstone Railway finally closed on June 13th, 1929.

The scattered hamlet of Thorgill, founded on a small cluster of farmsteads, once lodged men working the nearby Sheriff's Pit mine (encountered near the end of the walk). Accommodation in the dale was so overcrowded that beds, it is said, were never cold as one shift replaced the next. There is limited roadside space, so car parking should be chosen carefully.

You start by walking north-east back towards Rosedale Abbey, but turn off left at the first right-hand bend on a lane down to Low Thorgill Farm. The gate ahead is marked 'Public Footpath' and leads you down a field, half-left, to a footbridge over Gill Beck. An ancient paved way, typical of many in this part of Yorkshire, takes you over the ensuing field to another footbridge and up to a gap in a hedge. Now on a rutted track swinging left, you emerge at a kissing gate by some lock-up garages; the lane joins Daleside Road at Hill Cottages, built for employees of East Mines.

You cross the road and climb the lane opposite, passing a house—the old 'Depot Cottage' at the erstwhile Rosedale Goods Station— beyond which a gate gives out to a muddy track. A coal tip was located here and to the left the old Goods Shed is still used. Chickens, sheep and dumps of sundry materials on waste land lend a desolate air to this once-important terminus known as Low Baring, home to railwaymen who lived in a long row of cottages until the line closed in 1928.

Beyond the ruined coal cells, you walk left of a high embankment onto the recognisable trackbed itself. It is, perhaps, pertinent to mention that while many people enjoy this walk into history, it is not a definitive right of way. Before long, an impressive bank of masonry arches appears on the right—ruins of the original sixteen 'Old Kilns'—topped by the crumbling stub of a ventilation chimney which served horizontal 'drift' workings below.

To reduce the transportable weight of ironstone, it was first roasted in these kilns. Water and carbonic acid gas were thus driven off—a process called calcination—but the ore was not cooled, so metal-bodied wagons were necessary. Vast quantities of calcine dust waste accumulated below the kilns; its rich iron-oxide content was recognised as a resource in its own right before the mines finally closed and it was removed for processing in nearby Middlesborough between 1920 and 1927.

More derelict masonry—the so-called 'New Kilns' and loading stages—is reached in less than half a mile, standing directly above Petch Cottage at an area known as High Baring. Still visible above are the multi-level sidings associated with East Mines.

Two arms of Gill Beck are crossed before the track passes the remains of Black Houses, once linesmen's cottages but now just end-walls and a chimney. Already the great basin of Rosedale Head stretches to the north; views are readily appreciated for the easy walking makes few demands. Continuing on its terrace in the dale side, the trackbed passes a bridleway descent left to Dale Head Farm, a possible short-cut via Moorlands Farm and valley tracks back to Thorgill. A sharp loop round craggy Nab Scar is followed by culverted embankments over Reeking Gill and the headwaters of the River Seven.

Swinging round the head of Rosedale, you will notice a perceptible gain in height as southerly progress is made. The going is quite rough in places where complicated engineering work had been necessary to accommodate the gradient and the ground has slipped away. Within a mile you have passed the brick ruin of a water tank and are walking parallel to the road along Blakey Ridge, no more than 250m from the Lion Inn.

This lonely hostelry was once patronised by workers from the numerous small coal pits in the vicinity—1:25,000 OS map shows a veritable peppering of them—as well as by ironstone miners. It is still popular with walkers, cyclists and motorists crossing these moors 1325ft (403m) above sea level.

A little further south, at 1200ft (366m) stood a small huddle of railwaymen's cottages called Little Blakey. From the nearby junction, the ironstone railway began a moortop course, looping north-west round the heads of Bransdale and Farndale without recourse to either bridge or tunnel. Beyond Bloworth Crossing, wagons laden with ore were lowered by cable down Ingleby Incline to join the main railway network at the foot of the escarpment. Foodstuffs, timber and oil were among other freight carried in by returning trains.

Following the trackbed down Blakey Ridge, we can ponder the daily life of railway crews and miners. Conditions on or near the bleak moortops were often severe, yet men from local villages walked to and from work over rough moorland paths in all weathers. Gales and rain were regular hazards, while heavy winter snowfalls sometimes blocked the entire system and brought mining operations to a standstill. The sheer audacity of the railway's course and the rigours endured by workers bear witness to the ironstone industry's vitality during the latter half of the nineteenth century.

In 2½ miles (4km) you reach Sledge Shoe Bents, site of a former reservoir supplying locomotives. Ignore a path down left to High House Farm, continuing instead for another mile to a path junction at Sheriff's Pit. Before turning north-east into the dale, some final notes about this important ironstone mine.

Sheriff's Pit was worked as a vertical shaft— like a conventional coal mine—though horizontal drifts and a tramway were also constructed in the dale side above Medd's Farm. All pithead winding gear was removed when the mine closed in 1911 and today only the fenced-off shaft and a gaunt trackside ruin remain.

To conclude the walk, you follow the steepening path left in a stream valley, diverting right above a rocky outcrop. Traces of a building and drift entrances can be found among the adjacent quarries and tips. Once through the intake wall, you walk on downhill with a wall to your left, soon arriving at Medd's Farm. Keeping right past the buildings (also a riding school and camp site), you will pick up the rough Daleside Road track which becomes metalled and enters Thorgill hamlet.

No longer the eyesore they once were, the thinly overgrown relics of a unique period in our industrial history succumb each year to the elements—part of the land's reversion to a natural state. Where air and water were once polluted and the by-products of mining littered the dale, there is tranquillity and a regeneration of flora and fauna. Ultimately few visible signs will remain so we can count ourselves fortunate to witness what tangible evidence there is and to be able to make that easy leap of imagination back into an era gone forever.

Facing page: **The old coaching road along the broad summit of Rudland Rigg — late summer.**

WALK 29: *West Gill, Rudland Rigg and Farndale Nature Reserve*

Terrain: Some rough moorside to attain Rudland Rigg, then good tracks, a little road walking and riverside field paths, which can be muddy.
Start/Finish: Low Mill car park. **Distance:** 6½ miles (10.5km)—allow 3½ to 4 hours. **Maps:** OS Landranger Sheets 100 and 94; Outdoor Leisure South-West sheet.

A profusion of wild daffodils carpeting the River Dove's banks in early springtime draws crowds of sightseers to Farndale. Indeed, many visitors will be content simply to wander along the riverside path and back again, admiring the blooms and, perhaps, occasionally raising their eyes to the surrounding moors. That would undoubtedly constitute a 'classis stroll', but to discover the relationship between dale and moortop and to savour the essence of each—setting one against the other—it is necessary to step out a little further.

Not everyone will be fortunate enough to visit Farndale during the few weeks when its daffodils are in full bloom, though even outside this period the river valley is a delectable spot. However, for the summer walker there are compensations. From mid-August onwards, Rudland Rigg and Blakey Ridge, which enclose this part of Farndale, are transformed by a glorious purple haze as heather and ling come into flower.

A narrow daleside road runs north from Gillamoor and drops to the hamlet of Low Mill. In April a one-way system is imposed to deal with the 'daffodil traffic'—particularly coaches—and extra fields are opened for parking; weekends then are especially busy, so be warned! For the rest of the year, because upper Farndale's roads lead past farms to the dale head and no further, relatively few vehicles are encountered.

A nineteenth-century, water-driven corn mill gave Low Mill its name. It ceased grinding corn in the early 1930's but generated electricity for a further twenty years; although the building itself is much changed, the original leat supplying water can still be seen alongside the Dove. There is a small car park opposite Low Mill's post office, at first uphill on Daleside Road, and it is from here that we set off, at first uphill on Daleside Road. Directly ahead rears Horn End Crag, the southern buttress of Horn Ridge enfolding West Gill.

In 500m, a 'Bridleway to Rudland Rigg' sign points left on a track leading between Horn End Farm and cottages up to the right. Once through a gate, you are walking along a grassy bridleway above Crow Wood and the tree-lined bed of West Gill Beck. Cattle often congregate lazily round High Barn, beyond which you cross a curiously narrow field, negotiate a stile then, flanking trees on the left, walk over the beck's footbridge. Climbing gently out of the valley bottom over rough pasture it is necessary to keep left, parallel to a wall, before reaching a gate and bridleway sign. Soon after, the track swings right, uphill, and joins a thin trod from the left, rising to meet the wall above at a gate.

Garnets Crag and Double Crag guard the eastern edge of Rudland Rigg, forcing the path away from a direct ascent. Instead, it takes a gradually rising line over rugged, overgrown

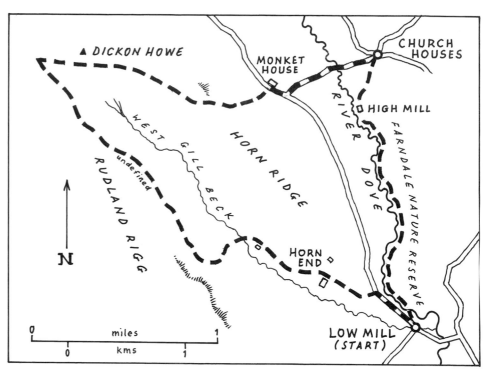

slopes. To begin with you are climbing beside a reedy stream, continuing ahead on marshy ground where it veers suddenly left. Although the path hereafter is more clearly defined underfoot—going north-west and parallel to the crags above—it is obscured by heavy beds of bracken in the summer. Nevertheless, it should present few difficulties and where the gradient eases there are opportunities to gaze back down the verdant West Gill valley, a remote little offshoot of Farndale. On the eastern valley side a bold patchwork of fields enclosed by dry-stone walls—reaching to the limit of usable land—lies beneath a long sweep of untamed moorland on Horn Ridge.

Despite more dense bracken (the scourge of walking in high summer!), the path persists, but when it reaches a sunken channel in the vicinity of disused tips and another stream bed, easier progress is made along the side banks. Maintaining its north-westerly course towards West Gill Head the way grows increasingly distinct and grassy. Double Crag, already superseded by less precipitous hillside, is now at your level and grouse butts on the left signal your imminent emergence onto Rudland Rigg.

Here a broad, stony track snakes across the undulating ridge top from one horizon to the other—hardly the most promising line for any thoroughfare, one might at first think. Yet dry ground along the watershed does avoid difficult and often boggy terrain on the moorsides and it is quite plausible that this north-to-south route has existed for some 2000 years, despite its obvious exposure to wind and weather. In more

recent times it became an important coaching road between Kirkbymoorside and Stokesley/Guisborough (witness the occasional milestones) and today provides a splendid moortop hike well above 1000ft (300m) for over 8 miles (13km).

Only rarely will you meet another soul in this expansive landscape, peopled, it seems, exclusively by sheep and grouse. Beside the old road, an infinity of stony heather is interspersed with water-filled hollows and isolated cairns or tumuli. This location—and there are many like it in the North York Moors—epitomises the qualities which attract lovers of solitude and unrestricted space. In all but the poorest weather these lonely heights, accessible only to the walker, are spirit-lifting, liberating, wildly beautiful yet rarely intimidating.

Turning right onto the old road, gently downhill for less than half a mile, brings you to a crossroads. To the left, over Ouse Gill and Shaw Ridge, lies Bransdale; ahead Bloworth Crossing and the Cleveland Hills escarpment. To the right another hard track traverses a vast expanse of heather above the source of West Gill Beck. The latter we take, heading east past stone-topped Dickon Howe standing 100m away in the heather.

Before long, as the track bends south-east, wide views open out over the tree patched, farm dotted flanks of upper Farndale. Subsidence has played havoc with the track as you plunge more steeply down through Monket House Crags. Sheep pasture leads to Monket House farmstead, derelict alas, and the daleside road. As you tread tarmac down over Thorn Wath Bridge to Church Houses, the walk assumes an altogether different complexion. Gone are far-reaching views, tussles with undergrowth and ankle-twisting terrain, their places taken by pastoral detail and a reflective amble on well walked riverside paths.

Farndale Church, restored in the early years of this century, dates from 1831 and stands a short distance east of the Feversham Arms. To enter the Farndale Nature Reserve, you take to a metalled lane opposite the pub and walk round by a hedge to High Mill. The little cluster of buildings once housed a blacksmith's forge and a corn mill powered by Blakey Gill, a tributary of the River Dove. Although standing idle for three-quarters of a century, the mill wheel and grinding machinery were still intact up to the late 1970s. At the time of writing, however, all that remains is a massive timber axle.

Our onward route now follows in the foot-steps of countless thousands who, during the brief duration of each year's flowering, flock to see Farndale's daffodils. Spread for some 6½

A summertime view over Farndale, before the descent to Church Houses.

miles (9.5km) along the River Dove's banks, their profusion is legendary but until 1955, when a local Nature Reserve was established to protect them, their very survival was threatened. Particularly after the advent of motorised transport earlier this century, people plundered the flowers indiscriminately and mercilessly. They came from the cities with their scythes and laundry baskets, carrying away blooms by the armful to sell in the streets and markets. In the process, flowers were trampled underfoot and without controls being imposed, the days of this annual explosion of colour and beauty were clearly numbered. The picking of daffodils within the

reserve is now illegal, ensuring their continuation for future generations to enjoy. Interestingly, according to some locals the blooms appear to have grown smaller in size since picking them stopped, suggesting, perhaps, that maximum density—a kind of saturation point—may have been reached.

Threading its way delightfully over stiles and round shady field corners alongside the meandering river, the way heads south through a succession of fields. It is easy walking, but after rain can become very muddy. In a little over a mile you cross a footbridge just below Low Mill, shortly afterwards arriving back at the car park.

What thousands flock to see — daffodil time in Farndale!

Facing page: **Bransdale Mill.**

WALK 30: *Upper Bransdale, Rudland Rigg and Bloworth Wood*

Terrain: Field paths, country roads and good moortop tracks. One main climb of about 500ft (152m). **Start/Finish:** Cockayne in Upper Bransdale.
Distance: 9 miles (14.5km)—allow 4 hours (5 hours if visiting Bloworth Crossing). **Maps:** OS Landranger Sheets 100 and 94; Outdoor Leisure South-West and North-West sheets.

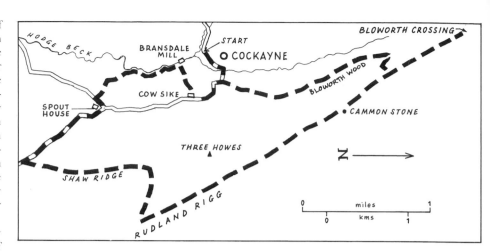

Upper Bransdale, 11 miles (18km) north of Helmsley, is as remote as anywhere in the North York Moors National Park. With its back to the highest tops around Botton Head, the upper dale, watered by Hodge Beck, lies closer to the northern escarpment than to the Vale of Pickering. But that is as the crow flies and the only way over those 3 miles (5km) is on foot. In common with other south-facing dales which thrust deeply into the moorland massif, Bransdale's narrow and sinuous roads—one from Helmsley and one from Gillamoor—service the farming community more than tourists. In my experience, sheep assume right of way over traffic!

Cockayne, where this walk begins, is a tiny settlement tucked into the northern corner of Bransdale. There are broad, grassy verges beside the dalehead road, but grazing cattle vandalised my car wing mirrors and aerial—behaviour which I trust is not habitual! The only alternative car parking is near the road junction at Spout House Farm, but care should be taken not to obstruct access.

Bransdale Lodge, set back above the road and out of sight from it, belongs to Lord Feversham; the nearby little chapel is of medieval origin. You start by walking east along the road, dropping over Bloworth Slack not far from its confluence with Badger Gill to form Hodge Beck, and continue round several acute bends to Cow Sike Farm. It is the first in a succession of farmsteads on Bransdale's eastern flanks: Toad Hole, Smout House, Yoad House, Spout House, Wind Hill, Goat Hill, Clegret and Lidmoor, the stuff of childrens' story books!

Crossing Cow Sike farmyard and passing through a gate in the right corner takes you down fields, over two ladder stiles and across reedy pasture drifted with buttercups in late springtime. A flight of stone steps leads to the mellow buildings of Bransdale Mill in its shady hollow by Hodge Beck. A mill, albeit a more modest structure, stood here as far back as the thirteenth century, though what we see today is the result of development by a William Strickland in the nineteenth century. His talented son Emmanuel, one-time vicar of Ingleby Greenhow, had the mill façades embellished with classical inscriptions, notably on the east wall.

Industrial buildings as substantial as these in so remote a location tend to take visitors aback. The complex was acquired by the National Trust in 1968 but renovation has been slow and halting. At the time of writing, however, a new water main is being laid and an access drive (previously a field track) is being bulldozed by the Royal Engineers. Restoration of old buildings is nearly always welcome, but I, for one, shall regret the inevitable 'tidying up', the taming of lush surrounding undergrowth and the loss,

perhaps, of echoes from the past which the mill's inaccessibility and secrecy served to heighten. But that, as they say, is progress!

After lingering here, you walk past outbuildings and on along the east bank of Hodge Beck into a field. Directions for following the beckside path are complicated by the usual intervention of gates and landscape detail. They are not relevant to an account of the walk and in any case are easily unravelled by vigilance and common sense. In less than a mile, a track rises to the dalehead road at a stile and you turn left between the lovely old barns of Spout House Farm.

At the road junction (an alternative starting point for the walk), turn sharp right, past a telephone kiosk, over the cattle grid and up the unfenced moor road for the better part of a mile (1.25km). The right of way shown on some maps cutting due east to Shaw Ridge would be useful if a trod existed on the ground, but it doesn't and the going is too rough to recommend. Topping a rise in the road, you will see a track off to the left at a 'No Access for Motor Vehicles' sign. This you follow on its northerly course along Shaw Ridge, the stony surface becoming sandy and grassier all the while. There are fine views in all directions, but especially west over the dipping moor road and Hodge Beck to the rugged slopes of Bransdale Moor.

You will pass a conspicuous cairn-topped mound, one of the many lesser ancient burial sites ignored by maps and consigned to anonymity. Grouse butts at a track junction ahead are typical of hundreds ranged over the central moors. Grouse shooting affects access for walkers during the autumn months. While it generates income for landowners and grouse populations are carefully managed, it has always struck me as a particularly 'unsportsmanlike' sport, running contrary to decent notions about the sanctity of life on this planet, whatever the species.

Here you make a right turn to cross the boggy

headwaters of Ouse Gill before swinging left along the old coaching road between Kirkbymoorside and Stokesley. We will meet this trackway on other walks, for it traverses more than 8 miles (13km) of moortop separating the long arms of Bransdale and Farndale. Its elevation at over 1000ft (300m) above sea level for much of its length avoids wet, difficult ground on the dalesides but must have been responsible for many an epic journey in the face of gale, mist or blizzard.

A marker stone colloquially marked 'Kirby Rode' focuses attention to detail in a world of big skies and heathery infinities. If your walk is blessed with clear air, look east for the distant Lion Inn on Blakey Rigg. Nearer at hand on the left are Three Howes tumuli, not themselves of prominent height but situated on a shallow summit of land and visible from afar.

At a cairn, a grassy track leaves east into Upper Farndale, while the overgrown track west from this junction would lead you to the road near Cow Sike Farm should a short-cut be required. Bloworth Wood is in sight ahead and excellent views south down Bransdale are opening up.

A broken shaft and socket stone are all that remain of Cockan Cross, though place names etched into its surface recognisably relate to the old coaching road. A kilometre farther on and probably erected as a waymark in prehistoric times, the curiously shaped Cammon Stone invites studied examination. It is an oddly cryptic monolith bearing an inscription in Hebrew on its west side, added in more recent times.

Soon the track gently begins to lose height and a left turn-off sweeps towards Bloworth Wood below. Providing the weather and your inclinations are both favourable, an easy half-mile (800m) stroll ahead will take you to Bloworth Crossing, an important intersection for moorland travellers, past and present.

During the latter half of the nineteenth century, trains laden with iron-ore plied between the Rosedale mines and Battersby near Middlesborough, although it is hard to imagine any railway operating in such high, wild country.

Steps are retraced and the track descended into Bloworth Wood, turning left along the forestry road. Until recently-planted spruce have grown higher—and that may not take long—there are good views of Cockayne Ridge and Bransdale Moor. Generally excluding light and creating an eerie gloom devoid of greenery, the communal huddle of conifers is not to everyone's liking. Nevertheless, your surroundings could hardly be more peaceful. Gates lead through a final belt of trees to the road above Hodge Beck and the walk's conclusion at Cockayne.

The moor road and distant Bransdale from Shaw Ridge.

WALK 31: *Urra Moor Dykes and Botton Head*

Terrain: Rough moortop paths and tracks, mostly stony but marshy in places. **Start/Finish:** Clay Bank Top. **Distance:** 6 miles (9.5km)—allow about 3 hours. **Maps:** OS Landranger Sheet 93; Outdoor Leisure North-West Sheet.

The B1257 from Stokesley to Helmsley cuts through an afforested but otherwise naturally formed declivity in the Cleveland Hills escarpment between Hasty Bank and Urra Moor. Here at Clay Bank Top there is generous car parking and many walkers use the relatively high road pass (842ft/257m) as a springboard for exploring moors to the east and west. Being on the main escarpment path, too, makes Clay Bank Top a potentially busy place, for numerous hikers pass by on such long-distance trails as the Cleveland Way, Lyke Wake Walk, Bilsdale Circuit and the White Rose Walk, among others.

This walk, however, leads you somewhat off the beaten track, though to begin and end with you are on the principle east-west pedestrian thoroughfare along Carr Ridge. Starting from the car park in a forest clearing below the road pass, where a minor road from Ingleby Greenhow joins the B1257, a forestry track heads south, parallel to the road, and joins the escarpment path. If parked by the roadside, you simply walk along to a waymarked gate on the left.

Climbing east, the way crosses a stile and increases in steepness up the rugged shoulder of Carr Ridge. At first you are hugging the perimeter of Greenhow Plantation, but this soon cuts away to the left and you are breaking through a rocky band in deeply eroded channels to attain the ridge's final slopes. From the wall here are superb views north beyond skeletal larches to Roseberry Topping, while behind you, to the west, the impressive bulk of Hasty Bank sweeps to its flat-topped summit.

There can be no mistaking the escarpment track—an old road from days long before motorised transport—as it continues over Urra Moor, eventually linking with other ancient trackways, notably one right along the crest of Rudland Rigg from Kirkbymoorside to Stokesley and Guisborough. We, however, now fork off to the right, following the conspicuous line of mound and ditch which contours then gradually dips along the western rim of Urra Moor.

Known locally as 'Cromwell's Trenches', these dykes, in common with most other similar features on the North York Moors, are hard to date with any certainty. They appear to pre-date recorded history (though it is thought some may be medieval in origin) and their precise function has never been satisfactorily explained. Most groupings of dykes are set back a short distance from abrupt, west facing scarp slopes and in this respect Urra Moor Dykes are typical,

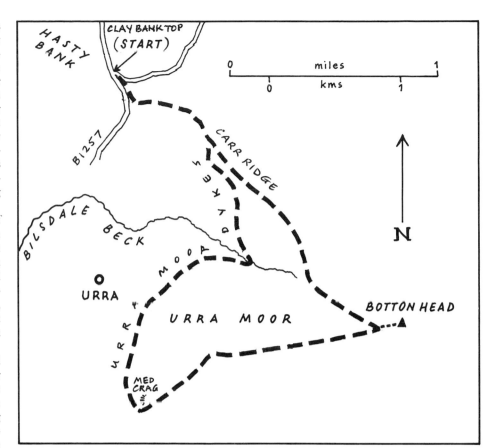

extending as they do for almost 3 miles (5km) along the eastern crest of Bilsdale.

Before you have followed path and earthworks for long, they cross the head of a ravine at Cowkill Well, one of the main sources of Bilsdale Beck. Spoil heaps from old jet workings are still evident on the hillside below workings which burrowed optimistically into these moorsides during the quest for that black relative of coal from which so many fashionable ornaments and jewellery were carved in the 1870s.

Having descended to round the stream valley, you now swing west for a while on rough, though mainly level ground. From this viewpoint, Carr Ridge and Hasty Bank form a dramatic skyline 'V' and the escarpment's profile is seen to good effect. Behind you the brooding convexity of Urra Moor rises to its unseen culmination but, for the present, eyes are more likely to be drawn to the valley farms of Upper Bilsdale over which you have a bird's eye view.

Reaching a wall above Urra hamlet, the path grows squelchier by the minute thanks to nearby springs. You have two alternatives for keeping dry feet: either stay close to the wall's firm base, or climb left round the marshiest area. Walkers wearing wellington or plastic boots will have the last laugh!

The going rapidly improves after some 300m and shortly, beyond where the wall dives down

to the right by conifer trees, Medd Crag appears up to your left. As crags go it is not especially prominent—more compelling is a track rising from Seave Green, an alternative starting point for this circular walk though 300ft (91m) lower than Clay Bank Top.

Onto this track you now turn, bidding farewell to the dykes which continue for about a mile further. Climbing towards the moortop, a broad, stony track is soon joined, striking a course north-east then east for approximately 1½ miles (2.5km) over the heathery expanses of Urra Moor.

Hill features which usually form pronounced shapes in views throughout this part of the North York Moors do no more than peep above the sprawling rim of this the highest ground in the National Park. When you arrive at a T-junction with the main path, and whether or not you detour a little way east to the OS pillar on a tumulus at Botton Head, 1490ft (454m) above sea level, views are extensive rather than interesting. Only from Ingleby Bottom, below the escarpment, does Urra Moor assume its true stature. Nevertheless, the situation should not be denigrated: after all, fresh air and wide horizons are in themselves often reward enough!

Turning north-west along the much-trodden, stony way, height is steadily lost and in clear visibility you will see the pale scar of a track thread-

Facing page: **Boundary stone on Urra Moor.**

ing along the summit of Carr Ridge in the distance. Numerous boundary stones are passed, often inscribed with the initial letters of parish or landowner whose territory they define.

In about a mile, you level off then rise slightly to meet a wall on the right: ahead lies the outward path which you walked earlier. The descent of Carr Ridge always seems much more entertaining and this must be attributed to the views which you now confront, supplanting a preoccupation with climbing which tends to monopolise the ascent. It is but a few minutes' work to drop down to the road; if you've time and energy to spare, why not tackle the steps opposite and romp up Hasty Bank whose strikingly impressive flanks you have just been admiring?

Facing page: **Sunset over long moorland horizons.**

Hasty Bank (centre) and Carr Ridge (right) from the Dyke path above Cowkill Well.

LONG-DISTANCE AND CHALLENGE WALKS

There are two very good reasons why the North York Moors lend themselves so well to long-distance and challenge walking. First, they offer richly varied scenery—dale, upland and coast—free from undue remoteness or technically difficult ground. Second, they are readily accessible to large centres of population such as York, Middlesborough and Teesside, as well as to coastal towns. Road and rail links from elsewhere in the country are reasonable too, though not everywhere in the National Park itself is served by public transport.

A distinction must be made at the outset between long-distance footpaths (both official and recreational), Challenge Walks, and Walking Events.

Britain's official Long-Distance footpaths have been designated such by the Countryside Commission and are suitably waymarked with signposts and acorn symbols. An official guide is normally available for such footpaths, but within the North York Moors only the Cleveland Way qualifies. There are, however, many long-distance recreational paths which have been

instigated by local authorities, voluntary bodies or even individuals. These routes follow existing rights-of-way but are not universally waymarked and guides vary from A4 leaflets to published books.

Challenge Walks may be attempted at any time but do embody a sporting element: to earn the certificate or badge awarded by a walk secretary, you much complete the route in one go, sometimes within a given time limit. There is, of course, nothing preventing you following a Challenge Walk at your own pace if you like the look of it.

Organised Walking Events are held on specific dates throughout the yearly calendar and invariably entail either walking against the clock, or against fellow participants, or both! Entry is by application form with accompanying fee and a maximum number of competitors is usually set beforehand. Rules govern your conduct through checkpoints and also relate to equipment carried, ensuring optimum fairness and safety. While not everyone's cup of tea, the proliferation of Events reveals their great

popularity.

Some walks from all three categories span only part of the North York Moors on their course to or from the Wolds and other adjacent areas, thus falling outside the scope of this book. It is not my intention, either, (with one exception) to feature the 20 or so specialised Walking Events which, while perhaps being classics of their kind, inevitably place more emphasis upon a walker's performance than upon a considered appreciation of his surroundings.

So we are left with long-distance Recreational Paths and 'anytime' Challenge Walks, of which 15 occur in the National Park. It would seem churlish to judge some walks of lower calibre than others: their diversity, in any case, makes comparisons difficult. Equally, there is insufficient space to do more than sketch in outlines of routes and give their vital statistics. Many are admirably described in publications available at Information Centres, bookshops, or from the organisers themselves and these are mentioned where known. After the Cleveland Way, walks appear in alphabetical order.

The Cleveland Way

Start: Helmsley.

Finish: Filey Brigg.

Distance: 93 miles (150km)—allow about a week's walking.

Maps: OS Landranger Sheets 93, 94, 99, 100 and 101. OS 1in to 1 mile Tourist Map for overall planning.

Details: Badge available from the Lyke Wake Club, Goulton Grange, Swainby, Northallerton, DL6 3HP (sae): Publications include: *The Cleveland Way* by A. Falconer (HMSO 1972); *The Cleveland Way and Missing Link* by M. Boyes (Cicerone Press 1989).

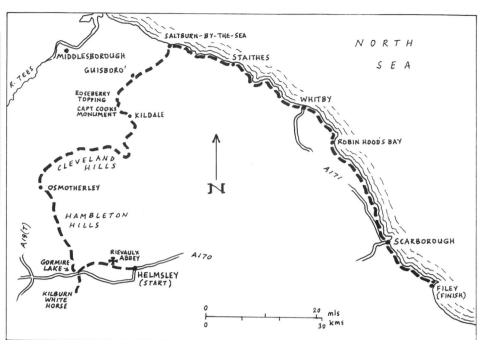

After almost 16 years of planning and access negotiations by the National Parks Commission and local authorities, the Cleveland Way opened officially in May 1969. The attractions of long-distance walking had already been acknowledged by the establishment of the Pennine Way, and the Cleveland Way immediately proved a worthy addition to what has now grown into a lengthy list of routes.

In truth, long walks had been undertaken over the moors and coast by individuals and groups, certainly for 15 years or more before the Cleveland Way became 'official' and probably for the best part of half a century. The trail's great appeal lies in its variety of natural scenery and in the tapestry of detail featuring many stages in man's history with which the walker is confronted. Thus, while lovers of landscape are treated to heather moorland, rocky escarpment, forest, lakes and Heritage Coast, those fascinated by our past can peruse Bronze Age tumuli, ancient trackways, monuments, old mine and quarry workings, disused railway lines and notable religious buildings.

Throughout its usually clockwise arc from Helmsley to Filey Brigg, the well waymarked trail stays, for the most part, within the National Park. A week's hiking is generally considered par for the course, though you could spend longer exploring a wealth of interest off the main path. If, on the other hand, you are fit and in a hurry, a few days would suffice, though adverse weather can always wreck the best laid plans.

Accommodation is more plentiful in some places than in others, so some advance thought is required, even for backpackers: most moorland is in private ownership and pitching 'wild' is to be discouraged. However, a growing number of farms take lightweight campers and there are youth hostels at Helmsley, Saltburn, Whitby, Boggle Hole and Scarborough. Elsewhere, bed and breakfast establishments provide the necessary shelter and home comforts.

A detailed description of the entire Cleveland Way would not only fill a disproportionately large space in this book but would duplicate information already given in shorter walks which coincide with it. Nevertheless, a route of such importance to the North York Moors cannot be dismissed in the foregoing paragraphs alone and I hope the following summary will whet the appetites of those who have not yet tackled it, as well as rekindling feelings of appreciation and achievement for those who have.

To add colour to a potentially rather bland catalogue of features encountered along the way, this summary recounts a personal journey made in recent years.

Stage 1—Helmsley to Sutton Bank

My companion and I arrived at Helmsley in mid-afternoon; it was early April, Eastertime, and already the village was chock-a-block with

The National Park Information Centre on Sutton Bank.

tourists—not at all the sleepy backwater we had expected.

Big rucksacks containing lightweight camping gear distinguished us from other strollers on the path towards Rievaulx Abbey; the going was pleasantly gentle along field edges and down through woods bright with violets, primroses, coltsfoot and wood anemones. Rievaulx Abbey was hugely impressive—a symphony of arches, soaring walls and ornate carving and an hour passed unnoticed before we slipped away along the lane and up to Bungdale Head Farm. Determined to secure a first night's pitch without complication—even if it was off route—we had telephoned ahead.

Woken by the dawn chorus and nearby sheep, we set off early to rejoin the path along by Spring Wood lakes, reflecting budding trees in their still green waters. Then it was up onto the Hambleton Hills plateau to Cold Kirby, down damp fields and along to the Hambleton Hotel. Suddenly breezy and cold, our arrival at the escarpment had us donning cagoules and woolly hats.

Stage 2—The Hambleton Hills

Views west from the scarp are legendary. The distant Pennines are often a centrepiece, but today's air was soft and vaporous. Nonetheless, Roulston Scar and Gormire Lake were visible and White Mare Crag reared above slopes orange-brown with winter's dead bracken. Along the escarpment past High Barn, you are skirting arable fields above a wooded drop.

We found a spring and enjoyed lunch on a sunny bank. The Hambleton Drove Road, broad and stony from centuries of use by man and beast, carries you along through a conifer plantation and out onto Little Moor; burned, blackened heather stretched for miles to the east. Grassier further on, the old road is used for galloping horses and we encountered the first fellow walkers since Sutton Bank.

From Black Hambleton's summit—culmination of the Hambleton Hills—views opened out across the Vale of Mowbray in thinning haze. Steeply downhill (gradients had been conspicuous by their absence so far) the Drove Road is heavily grooved by erosion from boots, tyres and rainwater. At a corner of the moor road to Hawnby you strike off down Oak Dale, past two small reservoirs and soon reach Osmotherley. We camped at the site above the village, thoroughly attuned now to the smells, sounds, colours, textures and forms of a landscape about to erupt into springtime vigour.

Stage 3—The Cleveland Hills Escarpment

The night was bitterly cold and frost armour-plated the tent flysheet; wearing all our clothes had scarcely kept us warm. After stocking up with provisions from the General Store, and a warming coffee at the pub, we climbed through South Wood to the British Telecom aerials and the trig pillar on Beacon Hill. Haze once again veiled distant views, the Cleveland Hills mere dim silhouettes, but such weather is universally preferable to wind and rain!

Schoolchildren on a field trip flocked along the forestry road through Coalmire Plantation. Beyond the abrupt descent into Scugdale we found heavy, cloying mud on the path towards

Arable farming at 1000ft (305m) on the Hambleton Hills.

Huthwaithe Green and were ready for a lunch break among old ironstone spoilheaps near the hamlet. Fortified by food and warm sunshine, we attacked the stiff climb onto Live Moor, relishing fine conditions for the harder walking ahead.

Carlton Moor, monopolised by its Gliding Club airstrip, seemed desecrated—a wasteland— but so was its northern slope, churned into a muddy desert by motorcycle scrambling bikes. No-one was around that day, the moors peopled only by grouse and punctuated by a scattering of ancient boundary stones and Bronze Age 'howes'.

Loins were girded up for the ascent to Cringle End with its stone seat and viewing table. Clouds had denied us the previous sunshine's

Above: **Gormire Lake and the Vale of Mowbray from the Hambleton escarpment.**

Left: **At the topograph on Cringle End.**

Facing page: **A last look back to the Cleveland Hills escarpment before descending off Battersby Moor to Kildale.**

warmth and it felt penetratingly cold, though visibility from the craggy escarpment had improved. You drop and climb, this time onto Cold Moor, then the process is repeated, including a scramble through The Wainstones (awkward with large packs) onto Hasty Bank.

Decision time, for once past the B1257 at Clay Bank Top, overnighting and obtaining fresh water would be problematic until Kildale was reached, some 6 miles (9.5km) ahead. Carrying 30lbs apiece up and down the switchback escarpment had been enough for one day, so we dropped to West Wood Farm, bought milk and eggs and pitched among a flock of pea-hens!

It rained all night and next morning we slithered up the muddy path onto Carr Ridge in driving mist. By 9.15 am we had passed Botton Head on Urra Moor, highest point on the North York Moors, and the sun had broken through. On Greenhow Moor you meet the stony coaching road from Rudland Rigg by an old wayside cross and thereafter the descent to Kildale was uneventful in improving weather, interrupted

only by stopping for a brew and a snack. That morning we had seen not another soul.

Stage 4—To the Coast

We provisioned at Kildale's friendly little post office/store and were off onto Coate Moor, through the plantation and on to Captain Cook's Monument. Down at the car park, family groups were playing cricket and we became their lunch time spectators! Despite lowering skies, we did make the almost obligatory detour up Roseberry Topping, its distinctive profile having been in view all day. Summit rocks and the trig pillar on this most accessible hill were covered with graffiti.

When sweat had dried, the climb was reversed and progress resumed over Hutton Moor. Desperate for a drink—we had passed no water all day—we were begrudgingly allowed to pitch at Codhill Farm: not all farmers are favourably disposed towards backpackers! Night provided a sound picture of surrounding countryside—bird scarers, owls, grouse, barking dogs, cows,

the distant rumble of traffic and, finally, heavy rain drumming on the tent fabric.

Morning saw the moors shining dark with moisture. The stretch of way from Guisborough Moor to the coast is the least attractive; a boot-clogging tramp over farmland and old quarries. Above Skelton, having escaped the jaws of a wrathful Jack Russell, we sat on a bench for a garibaldi and chatted to an elderly local; he rued the passing of the meadows and hedges, hares and skylarks of his youth, roundly blaming 'insecticides and lunatics'!

Saltburn greets you with its ornamental gardens and the clouds had cleared to balmy April sunshine. It is a strangely engaging town of faded Victorian splendour and we decided to dry out at a bed-and-breakfast for the coastal stage ahead.

Stage 5—Heritage Coast

That evening we enjoyed exchanging chat with two other walking couples. The snow showers forecast turned up on cue next morning and the

cold had us ensconced in cagoules and over-trousers. After 4 days inland, the coastal scenery seemed wild and animated—even Skinning-grove's derelict jetty echoed the weather's mood. Past tractors and pigeon lofts we set off to climb Boulby Cliff, loftiest on this seaboard, with a piercing wind behind us and exhilarating views all round.

Fish and chips at Staithes hardly did that delightful fishing village justice, but it was a day for walking not browsing. The tide was in at Runswick Bay, even the beach café was closed until the following day (Good Friday), a penalty for walking out of season. Awesome waves were breaking far out into the bay and along the beach head, forcing us to await a clearance. Eventually the seas ebbed and we hurried past Hob Hole in wind-blown salt spray, up to clifftop Kettleness and called it a day at Deepgrove Farm. A hedge sheltered our tent from the stiff northwesterly that had bullied us all day.

Following another cold night, we continued along the disused railway trackbed to vast alum quarries from the last century around Sandsend Ness. All morning, sea views had been dramatically beautiful. A favourable low tide allowed us to walk the sands right along to Whitby's harbour. There is much to see in this fascinating port: fish quays and moored craft, the Abbey, Frank Meadow Sutcliffe's photographs, the Pannett Museum and lots more. A second breakfast was consumed and after relishing the hustle and bustle of civilisation, we took our leave.

Straightforward enough, if near the precipitous edge in places, the clifftop walk to Robin Hood's Bay was soon achieved, the quaint village itself thronged with visitors. Wooden walkways over landslipped cliffs lead on and you drop to Boggle Hole before the long pull up to Ravenscar, with its Geological Trail and spectacular vistas over a rock-scarred shore. We pitched under a wall at Church Farm.

Facing page, above: **Old Saltburn and Hunt Cliff.**

Facing page bottom: **Looking back along the coast from Warren Cottages.**

Below: **Staithes — often besieged by a stormy North Sea.**

130

Next day the wind had abated and we trod the seaward fringe of a pastoral landscape. Hayburn Wyke's little beach waterfall proved an idyllic spot for a brew and snack, then it was up through Nature Reserve woodland and along to Cloughton Wyke. Scarborough Castle beckoned from its distant headland but we had picnicked near Scalby before finally arriving at the concrete, the crowds and the amusement parks of this popular East Coast resort. Scooter-borne mods had taken over the town for an Easter rally and we were glad to leave the undercurrent of violence behind: we learned later that 130 'mods and rockers' had been arrested over the Bank Holiday!

A cuppa at the Spa Café and, though tired by now, a decision to press on was made. The final miles past sprawling holiday amenities contrasted starkly with previous days of gloriously unfettered coast, but eventually things improved and Filey Brigg in the gathering dusk yielded a fitting climax. Footsore but content to have completed a memorable trek, we caught a late train, homeward bound.

Note: For those wishing to return on foot to Helmsley, a 'Missing Link' has been devised. First walked in 1975 by its originator, Malcolm Boyes, it leaves the coast north of Scarborough, crossing moors and forest in a 50 mile (80km) westward line, turning the Cleveland Way into a circular trail.

Full details can be gleaned from the appropriate guidebook (see 'Details' above), but in summary the way leaves the coast at Crook Ness, passes through Broxa Forest and along the ridge of Crosscliffe to Saltergate. It then passes the Hole of Horcum to Levisham and Stape, through Cropton Forest to Lastingham and Hutton-le-Hole, the final section being through Farndale and around Birk Nab to descend Riccaldale to Helmsley. The walk is usually undertaken in two or three days, with stops at Lockton youth hostel or Levisham and around Hutton-le-Hole.

Left: **Classic sea views from high cliffs south of Ravenscar.**

131

The Bilsdale Circuit

Start/Finish: Newgate Bank car park, north of Helmsley (564 890).
Distance: 29 miles (47km) plus 4000ft (1219m) of ascent.
Type of Walking: Strenuous, high-level moorland with several steep climbs and often off the beaten track. A little road walking. Superb views.
Maps: OS Landranger Sheet 100; Outdoor Leisure South-West and North-West sheets.
Details: Sae to Mike Teanby, Old School House, Village Street, Adwick le Street, Doncaster DN6 7AD. Booklet *The Bilsdale Circuit* published by Dalesman Books (1981). Badge and certificate on completion, but no time limit.

Mike Teanby inaugurated this route in 1977 on behalf of the North Yorkshire Long Distance Walkers Association. Over the ensuing years it has become a firm favourite with small groups who, above all, enjoy getting away from it all into unspoiled environments and who have the necessary resources with which to meet the challenge of this demanding hike. As well as appearing in the Events calender, the Bilsdale Circuit has become a popular alternative to the over-used Lyke Wake Walk.

From Newgate Bank the route describes a clockwise circuit of the moors flanking Bilsdale. Strategic points along the way include:- Moor Gate, High Thwaites, Carlton Bank, the Cleveland Hills escarpment to Hasty Bank, Urra Moor Dykes, Stump Cross, Bonfield Gill, and Roppa Wood.

The Crosses Walk

Start/Finish: Goathland Village Hall (830 012).
Distance: 54 miles (87km).
Type of Walking: Varied terrain encompassing moortop, daleside and valley bottom.
Maps: OS Landranger Sheets 100 and 101; Outdoor Leisure West and East sheets.
Details: This is a 24 hour Challenge Event held each July, usually on the first Saturday after the Lyke Wake Race and Osmotherley Gala. However, it also makes a fine, multi-day expedition. Sae to Mrs B. Hood, 21 St Peter's Street, Norton, Malton, North Yorkshire. Book *The Crosses Walk* by Malcolm Boyes, a Dalesman Paperback. For participants in the Event, there are badges, certificates and trophies to be won.

Pioneered in 1971 by a small group of enthusiasts (including Malcolm Boyes), the walk was given

Top: **Looking back to Hasty Bank from Urra Moor Dykes on the Bilsdale Circuit.**

Bottom: **Malo Cross on the Crosses Walk — an enigmatic landmark.**

to the Scarborough and District Search and Rescue Team; all proceeds from the Event go towards their running costs. Needless to say, it is a very long hike indeed, taken in one bite, but manned checkpoints and safety precautions ensure everyone has a fair chance of completing the course.

Its great appeal as a more leisurely exercise lies in the visiting of 13 moorland crosses—an opportunity to become acquainted with these enigmatic landmarks and the ancient trackways alongside which they stand.

The route starts west to Botton Cross, Fat Betty (White Cross) and the two Ralph Crosses, south to Ana Cross, High and Low Crosses, north-east to Mauley Cross, Malo Cross and Lilla Cross. From Postgate Cross the walk swings west back to Goathland via John Cross and York Cross.

The Eskdale Way

Start/Finish: Dock End, Whitby.
Distance: 82 miles (132km).
Type of Walking: Moortop and valley paths through fields, riverside pasture and woodland. Numerous ascents and descents.
Maps: OS Landranger Sheet 94; Outdoor Leisure North-East Sheet.

Details: For accommodation list, sae to the walk's originator—Louis S. Dale, 10 Mulgrave View, Stainsacre, Whitby YO22 4NX. Booklet *Eskdale Way* published by Dalesman Books (1983). No badge or certificate for completion.

Moving from valley bottom to moortop and back again, this circular route embraces the magnificent country around the River Esk from Whitby to Kildale. Many attractive villages are passed but accommodation is in short supply in some places, so be prepared to detour or extend the day's mileage.

Strategic points along the way include:-Sleights Moor, Grosmont, Goathland, Simon Howe, Wade's Causeway, Egton Bridge, Fat Betty and Ralph Cross, Westerdale, Baydale Abbey, Kildale, Commondale, Castleton, Danby, Lealholm, Glaisdale, Aislaby and Ruswarp.

The Esk Valley Walk

Start: The source of the River Esk near Esklets in Upper Westerdale (675 016).
Finish: West Pier, Whitby.
Distance: 30 miles (48km).
Type of Walking: Mainly low-level over easy terrain, though muddy in wet weather.
Maps: OS Landranger Sheet 94; Outdoor

Several long-distance routes take in Ralph Cross, adopted as the National Park's logo.

Leisure North-East sheet.
Details: Booklet *The Esk Valley Walk* published by the North York Moors National Park (1982), available from the National Park Information Service, The Old Vicarage, Bondgate, Helmsley YO6 5BP. No badge or certificate for completion.

Following the River Esk from its source high on Westerdale Moor to the North Sea at Whitby, the Walk passes through a pastoral landscape on field paths, tracks and country lanes. In fact, the route comprises 10 shorter walks joined together and thus forms the basis for either a long hike of 30 miles (48km) or a number of easier stages broken up by taking overnight accommodation. British Rail's Esk Valley line increases the scope for walking and return by train.

The trail is suitable for families and the less energetic and is waymarked where necessary with a leaping salmon emblem, in addition to the conventional footpath and bridleway signs. Strategic points along the way include:- Castleton, Danby, Beacon Hill and Brown Rigg End,

Lealholm, Glaisdale, Egton Bridge, East Arncliff Wood, Grosmont and Ruswarp.

The Hambleton Hobble

Start/Finish: Osmotherley (456 972).
Distance: 30 miles (48km) plus 2500ft (762m) of ascent.
Type of Walking: Mainly little-used field paths, but numerous ascents and descents involved along the Hambleton Hills escarpment.
Maps: OS Landranger Sheets 100 and 99; Outdoor Leisure South-West sheet.
Details: Sae to the originator—P.A. Sherwood, Wits End, South Kilvington, Thirsk YO7 2NF. No time limit.

The Hambleton Hobble clockwise circuit, devised to relieve the hard pressed Lyke Wake Walk, connects village pubs at Osmotherley, Scawton and Nether Silton—a concept that will appeal to everyone who enjoys partaking of refreshment and conviviality along the way!

Strategic points include :- Robinson's Cross, Arden Hall, Murton Grange, Old Byland, Wethercote Lane, Hesketh Hall, New Kepwick and Over Silton.

The Lyke Wake Walk

Start: Sheepwash (or Old Quarries) car park, north-east of Osmotherley (470 994).
Finish: Raven Hall Hotel, Ravenscar (980 018).
Distance: 40 miles (64km) plus 5000ft (1524m) of ascent.
Type of Walking: A high-level moors traverse and a serious undertaking, especially in poor weather, though on well trodden paths most of the way. Many ups and downs.
Maps: OS Landranger Sheets 99, 93 and 94; Outdoor Leisure all 4 sheets; 1in Tourist Map of the North York Moors.
Details: Sae to the Lyke Wake Club, Goulton Grange, Swainby, Northallerton DL6 3HP. Booklets *the Lyke Wake Walk* and *The Lyke Wake Way*, both by Bill Cowley, published by Dalesman Books (1983). Successful crossings in under 24 hours are rewarded by various orders of membership, such as 'Dirgers' or 'Witches', according to total number of crossings achieved. Send 20p and sae to above address for each crossing reported to receive a Condolence Card and entry in record book. A free leaflet on Moorland Safety is available from National Park Information Centres, or sae to the National Park Information Service, The Old Vicarage, Bondgate, Helmsley YO6 5BP.

The North York Moors' classic challenge! Pioneered by Bill Cowley in 1955, the Lyke Wake Walk started as a light-hearted, old fashioned funeral wake. It became undoubtedly the best known and most attempted long-distance route over the North York Moors. When the originator and his companions first

prospected the route 35 years or so ago, much of it was undefined across vast expanses of featureless heather moorland (it is still marked thus on the 1in Tourist Map). Since then, feet by the hundreds of thousands have tramped the same way, resulting in serious erosion, especially in the central peaty sections which coincide with other popular walks. For this reason, the National Park authorities are asking for parties attempting the Lyke Wake Walk to be kept small (10 or under) and to walk in single file wherever possible. Larger groups—such challenges

Many long-distance and Challenge walks in the National Park — including the Lyke Wake Walk — traverse the spectacular Cleveland Hills escarpment.

A walker on the Newtondale Trail near Levisham.

often attract those sponsored for charities—should find the recently introduced Shepherds Round or the Hambleton Hobble worthy alternatives.

To minimise night-time disturbance to residents of Osmotherley, not to mention problems of litter and vehicle parking, the start was shifted from Beacon Hill down to Sheepwash car park at the north-eastern end of Cod Beck Reservoir.

Thorough preparation and meticulous plan-ning will enhance your chance of making a successful crossing but the difficulties of this and other strenuous routes should never be underestimated. Experiences range from exhilarating, fine-weather romps to grim battles against the elements; whatever conditions are encountered, your fitness will be tested. It goes without saying that you should be properly clothed and equipped, aware of the weather forecast and that your walk plan is known by others in case of emergency.

Strategic points along the way include;- Huthwaite Green, the Cleveland Hills escarpment to Hasty Bank, Bloworth Crossing, Ralph Crosses, Trough House, Hamer, Wheeldale, Simon Howe, Eller Beck, Lilla Howe, Jugger Howe and Beacon Howes.

The Newtondale Trail

Start: Pickering (797 842).
Finish: Grosmont.
Distance: 20 miles (32km).
Type of Walking: Field paths and forest tracks with one or two moortop stretches.
Maps: OS Landranger Sheets 94 and 100; Outdoor Leisure South-East and North-East sheets.
Details: Sae to Mike Teanby, Old School House, Village Street, Adwick le Street, Doncaster DN6 7AP for A4 outline route sheet, to be used in conjunction with relevant OS maps. Badge and certificate on completion, but no time limit.

A 'must' for stream train enthusiasts and for those interested in geology, for the route shadows Newton Dale, a gorge excavated by glacial meltwater during the last Ice Age and now used by the North York Moors Steam Railway.

Some sections of trail lie close to the railway line, others take to forest and moorland tracks, crisscrossing the ravine three times. Marvellous contrasts are drawn between moortop, dale and woodland and although the trail is not generally arduous, its very length poses quite a challenge.

Strategic points along the way include:- Farwath, Levisham Road, Skelton Tower, Newtondale Halt, Simon Howe, Mallyan Spout, Beck Hole and the Murk Esk river.

The Reasty to Allerston 'Blue Man' Forest Walk

Start: Reasty Bank car park (965 945).
Finish: Allerston (877 830).
Distance: 16 miles (26km).
Type of Walking: Undulating, upland forest paths and tracks, muddy in places.
Maps: OS Landranger Sheet 101; Outdoor Leisure South-East sheet.
Details: Sae to the District Officer, Forestry Commission, 42 Eastgate, Pickering, Yorkshire, for an A4 route sheet. 'Blue Man' badge on completion (no time limit) is available from Dalby Forest Visitor Centre, Low Dalby, Pickering YO18 7LT.

Designed by the Forestry Commission to illustrate their work, the trail takes you through substantial tracts of conifer and broadleaved forest. Despite the tree cover, some excellent viewpoints are encountered.

The Rosedale Circuit

Start/Finish: Rosedale Abbey (725 959).
Distance: 37 miles (60km) plus 4000ft (1219m) of ascent.
Type of Walking: High level moorland tracks, valley field paths and a little moor road. A considerable number of ups and downs.
Maps: OS Landranger Sheets 100 and 94; Outdoor Leisure all 4 sheets.
Details: Sae to the Rosedale Circuit Secretary, Blackburn Welfare Society, Rambling Club, British Aerospace, Brough, North Humberside HU15 1EQ. Certificate on completion from Botton Village café.

Recommended as a 2-day hike, overnighting in the Westerdale area, this tough but inspiring circuit weaves round the very heart of the North York Moors. Often against the grain of the land, it links together Rosedale, Farndale, Bransdale, Westerdale, Danby Dale, Great Fryup Dale and Glaisdale, thus embracing some of the loveliest scenery the National Park has to offer. All monies received benefit the Camphill Village Trust for the mentally handicapped at Botton Village.

Strategic points along the way include:- Pike Howe, Church Houses, Rudland Rigg, Cockayne Ridge, Incline Top, Baysdale Abbey, Westerdale, Botton Village, Wood End and High Dale farms, Wintergill, Hamer House and Higher Row Mires.

Below: **On the Cockayne Ridge — Rosedale Circuit.**

The Lyke Wake path over Wheeldale Moor — a victim of its own popularity.

The Samaritan Way

Start/Finish: Guisborough (615 160).
Distance: 38 miles (61km) plus 4500ft (1372m) of ascent.
Type of Walking: High, lonely moorland, riverside and dale paths, disused railway trackbed and some moor road.
Maps: OS Landranger Sheets 94, 100 and 93; Outdoor Leisure all 4 sheets.

Details: Sae to Richard Pinkney, 11 Pine Road, Ormsby, Middlesbrough, Cleveland. Two classes of badge and a certificate on completion. All proceeds are denoted to the Teesside Samaritans. Twenty-four hour optional time limit.

Officially inaugurated by Lord Guisborough in 1978, the route takes its name from the organisation it supports. The walking is tough, involving rolling heather moor, lofty ridges, escarpment views and daleside fields, as well as a stretch alongside the River Esk. The Lion Inn, Blakey, provides an obvious refreshment stop at around the half-way mark.

Strategic points along the way include:- Highcliff Nab, Captain Cook's Monument, Kildale, Baysdale Abbey, Great Hograh Moor, Esklets, the Lion Inn, Rosedale Head, Trough House, Wood End Farm, Danby, Commondale and Hob on the Hill.

The Scarborough Rock

Start/Finish: Peasholm car park (035 897).
Distance: 26 miles (42km) plus 2000ft (610m) of ascent.
Type of Walking: Bay and cliff paths, woodland, riverside and dale.
Maps: OS Landranger Sheet 101; Outdoor Leisure South-East sheet.
Details: Sae to Mr M. Ellis, 77 Worthing Street, Clough Road, Hull HU5 1PP. Twelve hour time limit but no badge or certificate.

Launched by the East Yorkshire Group of the Long-Distance Walkers Association in 1982, the trail takes in Scarborough's twin bays and the coast to the north. Equally impressive are Forge Valley Woods and Hackness with its hall, village, park and lake. Secluded Low Dales and Whisper Dales lead to the Forestry Commission car park on Reasty Bank and country lanes return you to the cliff path via Burniston.

Strategic points along the way include:- Oliver's Mount, Seamer Beacon, Forge Valley Picnic Site, Hackness, Whisper Dales, Reasty Bank, Kirklees Farm and Burniston Cliff Top.

The Scarborough Samaritans

Start/Finish: Scalby (009 904).
Distance: 25 miles (40km) plus 1000ft (305m) of ascent.
Type of Walking: Field, riverside and cliff paths, disused railway trackbed and country lanes.
Maps: OS Landranger Sheet 101; Outdoor Leisure North-East and South-East sheets.
Details: Sae to Keith, The Samaritans, 35a St Nicholas Cliff, Scarborough. Twelve hour time limit but no badge or certificate.

Specifically designed to attract those who wish to support a very worthwhile cause, this circular route was established in 1984. All monies received support the Scarborough Samaritans Centre. In addition to this aspect, the walk includes some fine and varied scenery combining woodland, dale, riverside, moor and coast. Like several others, this itinerary is intended to relieve pressure from the over-used Lyke Wake Walk, though by comparison it is considerably tamer.

Strategic points along the way include:-

Forge Valley — visited by walkers attempting the Scarborough Rock.

Wrench Green, Langdale Bridge, Harwood Dale, the A171, Ravenscar, Hayburn Wyke and Burniston.

The Seahorse Saunter

Start; Kilburn White Horse (515 814).
Finish: Whitby's famous 199 steps—the top!
Distance: 43 miles (69km) plus over 5000ft (1524m) of ascent.
Type of Walking: Field paths, bridleways and paved packhorse paths crossing moors and dales.

Maps: OS Landranger Sheets 100 and 94; Outdoor Leisure South-West and North-East sheets.
Details: Sae to Stephen Watkins, 36 Barons Crescent, St Giles Park, Copmanthorpe, York YO2 3TZ—for route and accommodation lists. Badges available for all finishers but certificate only to those completing in 24 hours.

Longest of all the 'anytime Challenge Walks', the Seahorse Saunter was originally conceived in 1984 as a backpacking weekend. It rapidly became an alternative to the Lyke Wake Walk, however, and has gained in popularity since, with almost equal numbers of single day crossings and leisurely weekends being recorded. Completely traversing the moorland block, you can expect there to be numerous ups and downs, though the initial and final stages are less demanding.

Strategic points along the way include:- Cold Kirby, Newgate Bank, Rudland Rigg, Church Houses, Fryup Head, Egton Bridge and Grosmont.

The Shepherds Round

Start/Finish: Sheepwash (or Old Quarries) car park, north-east of Osmotherley (470 994).
Distance: 36 miles (58km) plus 5000ft (1524m) of ascent.

Above: **The Cammon Stone beside the Shepherds Round route over Rudland Rigg.**

Below: **The Kilburn White Horse — end of the White Rose Walk.**

Type of Walking: Footpaths, bridleways and tracks engirdling the main moorland block to north and south.

Maps: OS Landranger Sheets 100, 93 and 94; Outdoor Leisure South-West and North-West sheets.

Details: Sae to the Lyke Wake Club, Goulton Grange, Swainby, Northallerton DL6 3HP for route leaflet, accommodation and badges list. Gold badge available for a circuit under 24 hours, green for a longer circuit. (Optional 24 hour time limit.)

First suggested as the definitive alternative to the Lyke Wake Walk by Alan Neasham of Osmotherley, the Shepherds Round has been squarely adopted as offering good firm going for larger groups of walkers (unlike the Lyke Wake route). As a 24 hour Challenge it is strenuous and should only be attempted by experienced hill walkers who are properly equipped and prepared. Even as a 2 day expedition it will still stretch many hikers and a couple of stages are undefined, calling for navigational skills.

Strategic points along the way include:- Live Moor, Carlton Bank, the Cleveland Hills escarpment to Hasty Bank, Bloworth Crossing, Cockayne, Bonfield Gill, Fangdale Beck, Honey Hill, Hawnby, Kepwick Bank Top and Black Hambleton.

The White Rose Walk

Start: Newton-under-Roseberry (571 128).
Finish: Kilburn White Horse (514 813).
Distance: 31 miles (50km), with options for longer routes of 34 miles (55km) and 37 miles (60km). An ascent of 4000ft (1219m) involved.
Type of Walking: Escarpment tracks, paths, some moorland and dale; quite strenuous.
Maps: OS Landranger Sheets 93 and 94; Outdoor Leisure South-West and North-West sheets.
Details: Sae to Mr George Garbutt, 17 Kingsclere, Huntington, York YO3 9SF for details of route, badges etc. Booklet *The White Rose Walk* by Geoffrey White, published by Dalesman Books (1980). No time limit.

Named from linking the 'White' of Kilburn White Horse with the 'Rose' of Roseberry Topping in the country of the White Rose, the walk was first completed by the Yorkshire Wayfarers Rambling Club in June 1968. It represents a departure from the usual east-west crossing or circular routes; by using paths and old tracks along the Hambleton Hills and Cleveland Hills escarpments, views over moor and plain alike are outstanding. Of the three length options the shortest has proved most popular, both because of its more manageable distance and for the mid-way break at the Buck Inn, Chop Gate.

Strategic points along the shorter way include:- Roseberry Topping, Captain Cook's Monument, Kildale, Botton Head, Chop Gate, Head House, Whitestones and the Hambleton Drove Road to Sutton Bank.

Roseberry Topping — a conspicuous landmark at the start of the White Rose Walk.

APPENDIX

Useful Addresses

British Trust for Conservation Volunteers
36 St Mary's Street
WALLINGFORD
Oxon OX10 0EU

Camphill Village Trust
Botton Village
Nr. Danby
WHITBY
YO21 2NJ

Camping and Caravanning Club of Great
Britain
11 Grosvenor Place
LONDON SW1W 0EY

Cleveland Tourist Board
125 Albert Road
MIDDLESBROUGH
TS1 2PQ

Council for National Parks
45 Shelton Street
LONDON
WC2H 9HJ

Countryside Commission
John Dower House
Crescent Place
CHELTENHAM
GL50 3RA

Department of the Environment (Ancient
Monuments Commission)
25 Saville Row
LONDON
W1X 2BT

Forestry Commission District Office
42 Eastgate
PICKERING
North Yorks.

Long Distance Walkers' Association
Membership Secretary
Lodgefield Cottage
High Street
Flimwell
WADHURST
East Sussex TN5 7PH

Moors Centre
Danby Lodge
Danby
WHITBY
North Yorks.

National Trust
36 Queen Anne's Gate
LONDON
SW1H 9AS

Nature Conservancy Council
Archbold House
Archbold Terrace
NEWCASTLE-UPON-TYNE
NE2 1EG

North Yorkshire County Council
County Hall
NORTHALLERTON

North York Moors Association
7 The Avenue
Nunthorpe
MIDDLESBROUGH
TS7 0AA

North York Moors Historical Railway Trust
Pickering Station
PICKERING
North Yorks.

North York Moors National Park Informa-
tion Service
The Old Vicarage
Bondgate
HELMSLEY
YO6 5BP

Ramblers Association
1/5 Wandsworth Road
LONDON
SW8 2LJ

Royal Society for the Protection of Birds
The Lodge
SANDY
Beds. SG19 2DL

Ryedale Folk Museum
Hutton-le-Hole
North Yorks. YO6 6UA

Woodland Trust
Autumn Park
Dysart Road
GRANTHAM
Lincs. NG31 6LL

Yorkshire and Humberside Tourist Board
321 Tadcaster Road
YORK
YO2 2HF

Yorkshire Wildlife Trust and Yorkshire
Naturalists' Trust
10 Toft Green
YORK
YO1 1JT

Youth Hostels Association
Trevelyan House
ST ALBANS
Herts. AL1 2DY

A Country Code for the Moors

1   Guard against all risk of fire, especially on the moortops in summer. Inform the Police of any fire's location and do not attempt to fight it yourself unless it is small.

2   Keep dogs under close control, particularly near livestock.

3   Stay on public paths across farmland, unless re-routed round the edge of crops by a farmer. Where possible walk in single file.

4   Respect hedges, walls and fences by only crossing them at gates and stiles. Fasten all gates behind you.

5   If you encounter a grouse-shooting party on your route, wait until it is clear to pass, or turn back and choose another path. National Park Information Centres should have details of moors being used for shooting.

6   Pack your litter in rucksack or pocket and take it home: bottles, cans and plastic containers can kill wildlife.

7   Help to keep all water sources clean.

8   Avoid unnecessary disturbance to wildlife, plants and trees; take photos, not specimens!

9   Take special care walking or driving on twisting country roads: see and be seen. Many sheep are needlessly killed each year by careless motorists.

10 Respect the privacy of local residents and avoid noise disturbance, particularly early and late in the day.

11 Make every effort to obtain permission before pitching a tent.

12 Keep well back from the crumbling edge of cliffs along the coast, especially in windy weather, and know the tide times before setting off along beaches.

13 When parking on country roads, avoid causing inconvenience to passing traffic and farm vehicles.

WALKING LIBRARY

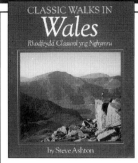

The Hill Walker's Manual
Bill Birkett

Over a three-year period the mountain rescue services had to deal with 2,799 casualties and 316 fatalities in mainland Britain. This book, which covers all walkers need to know about understanding the hills, equipment, clothing, navigation, walking techniques, survival and photography, is essential reading for anyone contemplat-ing walking in the hills.

128 pages, 32 pages colour, b&w photos, diagrams
£14.95

Classic Walks in Wales
Steve Ashton

Forty of the best walks in Wales, from lowland strolls for the family on holiday to longer walks for experienced hill walkers, to demanding mountain traverses. All walks have been graded to help selection and have been divided into areas.

Hardback, 144 pages, 72 in colour, black and white photos, maps
£16.95

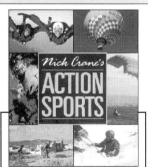

The Great Walking Adventure
Hamish Brown

"...a book to be treasured... an excellent buy for those who get their adventures in an armchair and those who use their feet."

232 pages, 8 in colour, maps **£9.95**

Walking In France
Rob Hunter

"A well thought out guide book which surely answers every question and covers every contingency facing a walker in France." *The Great Outdoors.*

224 pages, paperback, maps, line drawings **£4.95**

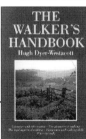

Classic Coastal Walks of Britain
Martin Collins

A selection of 40 of the finest walks situated along Britain's coastline. Every walk is in an Area of Outstanding Natural Beauty or covers Heritage Coast. Most are a good day's walk length (15 miles), a few taking 2 days. Maps and fact panels - highlighting location, distance, suitable maps and points of interest accompany each walk.

Hardback, 144 pages, 72 in colour, black and white photos, maps
£16.95

Classic Walks on the North York Moors
Martin Collins

A marvellous collection of 36 walks that together encompass all the magnificent features of this National Park area - the ancient burial chambers, hikes along old railway tracks past industrial relics, picturesque fishing harbours on the rugged North Sea coast. Rolling moorland, great sea cliffs and gentle pastoral dales are all here offering something for everyone.

Hardback, 144 pages, 72 in colour, black and white photos, maps **£16.95**

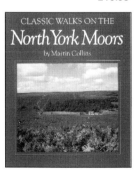

Nick Crane's Action Sports
Nicholas Crane

An up-to-the minute guide to all the most exciting adrenaline-inducing sports available today. Here you can enjoy the thrills of testing yourself on rock faces or white water; in deep and dark pot holes; on the depths of the sea bed or leaping off cliffs and mountains beneath a parachute. Over 20 sports covered.

Hardback, 132 pages, colour throughout
£14.95
Also available in paperback **£9.95**

The Walker's Handbook
Hugh Westacott

Three sections cover: Equipment and Walking Skills, The Legal Aspects of Walking, Where to Walk. The latter is mainly British based but also covers walking abroad. While it is written with the newcomer in mind, the more experienced walker will find the extensive bibliography, the OS sheet numbers and footpath guides most useful

312 pages, maps & diagrams
£12.95

Classic Walks in Southern England
Kev Reynolds

This book will open the eyes of all those cynics who dismiss the south as a tangle of motorways and urban sprawl. This collection of inspired essays and colour photos, describes walks through the woodlands of the New Forest, over the Downs and moors, round the coast and along the Thames; passing through some of England's prettiest villages.

Hardback, 144 pages, 72 in colour, black and white photos, maps **£16.95**

Classic Walks in the Yorkshire Dales
144 pages 72 pages colour, 72 pages b&w photos, maps **£16.95**

Classic Walks in the Lake District
160 pages 72 pages colour, 72 pages b&w photos, maps **£14.95**

Classic Walks in the Pyrénées
144 pages 72 pages colour, 72 pages b&w photos, maps **£16.95**

Classic Walks of The World
160 pages 80 pages colour, 80 pages b & w photos, maps **£14.95**

Classic Walks in Europe
Paperback, 160 pages, 80 pages colour, 80 pages b & w, maps **£9.95**

Classic Walks in Great Britain
Paperback, 184 pages, 80 pages colour, maps **£9.95**

Classic Walks in Scotland
Paperback 160 pages 72 pages colour, 72 pages b&w photos, maps **£9.95**

Classic Walks in France
136 pages 68 pages colour, 68 pages b & w, 20 maps **£14.95**

Size of all books: 250 x 207mm

All the books in this advertisement are available from leading bookshops, or, in case of difficulty direct from:
Cars & Trains, Boats & Planes (CATBAP) Bookshop, 15 Cowley Road, Oxford OX4 1HP   Telephone 0865 793553
Please send a cheque or Postal Order with your order, adding £1.00 (overseas £4.50) to the published price to cover post and packing.
All the prices quoted in this advertisement were correct at the time of going to press.

HAYNES

The Complete Transport Publisher
HAYNES PUBLISHING GROUP
SPARKFORD, NR YEOVIL, SOMERSET BA22 7JJ TELEPHONE (0963) 40635